TOMORROW'S HEROES

For People in Pursuit of a Difficult Dream

I0087719

Lou Heffernan

Peace Over Power™

Jupiter, Florida 33468 USA

Peace Over Power Publishing
PO Box 2424
Jupiter, FL 33468
www.PeaceOverPower.com

Peace Over Power™

Tomorrow's Heroes
(c) 2013 by Lou Heffernan

Library of Congress Control Number: 2013901517

Limit of liability/Disclaimer of Warranty:
This book and songs have been written to inform and educate the reader and reflect the opinion of the author. The author and publisher offer no guarantees about the effectiveness of this information and advise the reader to seek professional assistance.

Music Publishing Information: Songs can be accessed at SoundCloud.com or purchased at Amazon.com. Search for Lou Heffernan.
Copyright 2013 by Lou Heffernan. All rights reserved.
All songs by Louis Daniel Heffernan - ASCAP Member #1568650
Songs published by Lou Heffernan Music - ASCAP Member # 0046607
    American Society of Composers, Authors and Publishers (ASCAP)
    One Lincoln Plaza, New York, New York 10023

Available for purchase at Amazon.com.

Publisher's Cataloging-In-Publication Data   (Prepared by The Donohue Group, Inc.)

Heffernan, Lou.
    Tomorrow's heroes : for people in pursuit of a difficult dream / Lou Heffernan.

    p. : ill. ; cm. + digital sound files.

    Free audio downloads of original songs that accompany the book are available online at www.SoundCloud.com.
    Includes bibliographical references.
    ISBN: 978-0-9888473-0-9

    1. Goal (Psychology) 2. Success--Psychological aspects. 3. Achievement motivation.
I. Title.

BF505.G6 H44 2013
158.1

To the Reader,

Tomorrow's Heroes is a multi-media project designed to offer support and encouragement to people in pursuit of a difficult dream. Think of it as a toolkit to carry with you on your journey. To listen to recordings of the songs go to SoundCloud.com and enter "Tomorrow's Heroes" in the Track Search. If desired, the songs may also be purchased at Amazon.com.

My hope is that you will answer the call of your heart, step toward your passion, walk with determination, and seek a healthy balance for your life as you pursue your dreams.

About the author:

Lou Heffernan is the former Managing Editor of *American Songwriter Magazine* in Nashville, Tennessee. He is a professional member of the American Society of Composers, Authors and Publishers (ASCAP) as both a songwriter and a publisher. Lou has also worked within the health and wellness industry since 1981. His experience includes: being a Physical Education Department faculty member, a wellness professional, a Biofeedback Technician (stress management) and serving on the board of directors for numerous health and self-defense facilities throughout New England.

ACKNOWLEDGEMENTS

PHOTOS AND DRAWINGS
All photos, drawing and graphics are property of Lou Heffernan.
Thanks to Tippy Missick and Margie Noone for posing for photos.

CLIP ART
Clip Art from Adobe PageMaker 7.0: Mosquito

SONGS
To listen to songs go to SoundCloud.com and search for Lou Heffernan. Songs may be purchased at Amazon.com.

All songs were written, produced and sung by Lou Heffernan. The accompaniment for each song was created using Sony Acid Pro, a song construction software program. This software enables the user to assemble musical bits (or loops) into songs. I did not play any of the instruments but selected and assembled all the loops. I greatly appreciate all the musicians who make these libraries available to songwriters and producers. The following music loop libraries were used to produce this project.

Music Loop Libraries:

1. Acid (Sonic Foundry, Inc.)
2. Acid Essential Sounds (Sonic Foundry, Inc.)
3. Acoustic Guitar 1 (Power FX Loops)
4. Acoustic Guitar 2 (Power FX Loops)
5. American Piano (Doug Colosio, Sony)
6. Bass X (Sony)
7. Bradley Fish Restrung (Sony)
8. Bradley Fish Unstrung (Sony)
9. Cakewalk Plasma Loops (Twelve Tone Systems, Inc.)
10. Dr. Fink's Funk Factory (Sony)
11. Drums On Demand Bass Vol. 1 (Hobby Horse Productions, Inc.)
12. Drums On Demand Percussion (Hobby Horse Productions, Inc.)
13. Drums On Demand Vol. 1 (Hobby Horse Productions, Inc.)
14. Drums On Demand Vol. 2 (Hobby Horse Productions, Inc.)

15. Drums On Demand Vol. 4 Country & Crossover (Hobby Horse Productions, Inc.)
16. Electric Guitar (Smart Loops)
17. Electric Guitar Rock (Power FX Loops)
18. Guitar Studio (Brian Tarquin, Big Fish Audio)
19. Jade Hill: Rock/Pop Guitars (Sony)
20. Mellow Jazz/Funk Elements (Sony)
21. New York Dance (Sony)
22. Old School Funk Bass (Josquin Des Pres, Big Fish Audio)
23. Organ Donor (Joe Vitale, Sony)
24. Performance Loops Acoustic Guitars Vol. 1 (Big Fish Audio)
25. R&B Backline (Chuck Webb's Rhythm Section, Big Fish Audio)
26. Siggi Baldursson Pure Acid Drum Sugar (Sonic Foundry, Inc.)
27. Six-String Orchestra (Parthenon Huxley, Sony)
28. Songwriters Acoustic Guitar Companion (Leo Cavallo, Sony)
29. Sonic Excursions for Acoustic Guitar (J. Arif Verner, Sony)
30. Starvu Session Keys (Matt Fink, Sony)
31. Troy Klontz Rhythm & Twang (Sony)

Each song title is listed below followed by the corresponding loop library numbers used to produce that particular song.

Song Titles	Loop Libraries Used in Production
Don't Wrestle With The Road	6, 12, 13, 14, 16, 23, 30
Fill'er Up	11, 12, 13, 21, 22, 23
Have You Got What It Takes?	8, 11, 12, 13, 16, 18, 23, 27, 30
Keep Our Dreams Alive	6, 8, 9, 10, 11, 12, 13, 16, 17, 23, 27, 30
Never Let Go	1, 8, 10, 11, 12, 15, 16, 30
No Room For Negatives	6, 8, 11, 12, 13, 26, 27, 30
Raging Tiger Behind Paper Bars	5, 11, 12, 13, 31
Seems To Me	11, 12, 19, 28, 29
So Many Mountains	6, 10, 11, 12, 13, 16, 20, 21, 23
Somethin' Tells Me	6, 8, 10, 12, 13, 14, 16, 19, 23, 27
The Pearl	7, 8, 12, 13, 16, 23, 25, 27
The Spirit Lying Dormant	2, 11, 12, 13, 26, 28, 29
Stand Back	6, 12, 13, 16, 21, 26
Take 2 For U	8, 20
Tell Me What Life's About	2, 6, 12, 14, 23, 27, 30
Tomorrow's Heroes	2, 11, 12, 13, 19, 23, 28, 30

Dedicated to:

Grammy Dot, Gapey,
Mom and Dad

Thank you for your fighting spirit,
your giving nature, and your sense of humor.

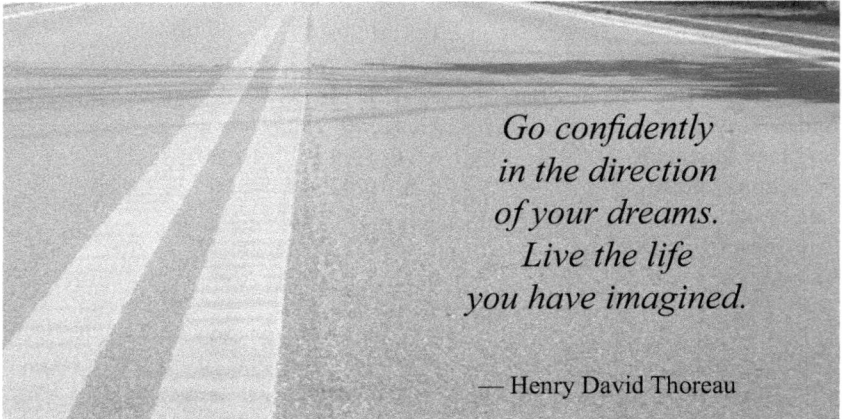

*Go confidently
in the direction
of your dreams.
Live the life
you have imagined.*

— Henry David Thoreau

TABLE OF CONTENTS

In someone's eyes,
I may never be anything more
than a dreamer.

In my eyes,
I can never settle
for anything less.

— LDH

INTRODUCTION

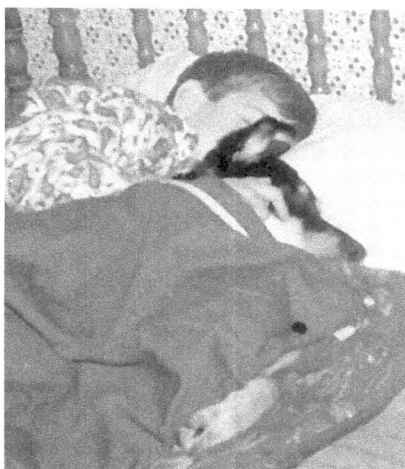

*In my dreams,
I was being encouraged
to follow my dreams.*

Photo: To avoid any confusion, I'm the one on the left. (Many years ago.)

When I was younger, I developed some unusual problems with my eyesight. Doctors were baffled by what was happening and concerned that I might be losing my sight. Obviously, this was a very difficult time in my life. One night, about six months after the onset of the problem, I awoke with an unusual phrase running through my mind. I found this amusing, but dismissed it and went back to sleep. For consecutive nights, I was again awakened by what I began to call, "Dream Messages." They seemed to be trying to encourage me to find the good in what was going on even though it was very difficult.

The difficulty of this situation forced me to take a hard look at myself, my life and my dreams. I thought about the things I wanted to do, the places I wanted to see, and the faces I wanted to memorize before it was too late. The possibility of losing my eyesight actually opened my eyes to so much that I had been overlooking.

After six years I began to wake up hearing these "Dream Messages" as songs in my head. Throughout my life I've returned to these songs for the support and encouragement they give me. My hope with this book and original songs is to share this support and encouragement with others in pursuit of their dreams.

Grow As You Go

Initially, it is likely that you will not possess all the skills needed to be successful at your dream. If you wait until you are totally prepared, you will probably never begin. Develop your skills along the way. Grow as you go.

— LDH

1

A Rumble Deep Inside

*Don't let the noise of other's opinions
drown out your own inner voice.
And most important, have the courage
to follow your heart and intuition.*

— Steve Jobs,
Co-Founder of Apple Computer

NEVER LET GO

I've got dreams I'll never let go
that this crazy world would suddenly know.
There's a chance for better times,
much more love, and peace of mind.

I don't care what you do to me,
in my heart I'm always free
and no matter what you say,
you can't take my dreams away.

Chorus:
No, no, no (No, no, no)
I'll never let go. (Never let go)
No, no, no (No, no, no)
I'll never let go. (Never let go)

I've got dreams I'll never outgrow,
that I've held inside from long ago.
Every dream I hold in my heart
keeps my life from fallin' apart.

I don't care what you do to me,
in my heart I'm always free
and no matter what you say,
you can't take my dreams away.

REPEAT CHORUS

'Cause no matter what you say,
you can't take my dreams away.

REPEAT CHORUS

I'll never let go. No, no, no, no
Never, never, never, never, never. Never let go.

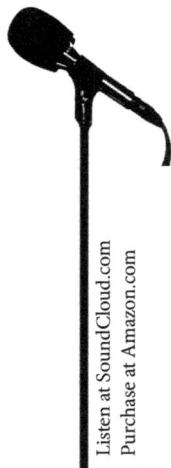

Listen at SoundCloud.com
Purchase at Amazon.com

SOMETHIN' TELLS ME

Learned my lesson long ago, I've got the chance to change.
So much of life out there waitin' for me to turn the page.
Each time I start to dream of all that I could be.
A gentle voice within says, "Find yourself set him free."

CHORUS:
Somethin' tells me it's alright.
Somethin' tells me I'm gonna make it.
Take each obstacle in stride.
If I fall at least I've tried.
Somethin' tells me it's alright.
Somethin' tells me I'm gonna make it.
Seeds of hope talkin' inside,
sayin', "Trust yourself . . . it's alright."

Somethin' happens every time there's a mountain to climb.
A rumble deep inside, says, "Take the first step . . . I'll drive."
I'll stumble, I'll falter when it's time to move.
Advancing toward tomorrow with plenty to gain,
not much to lose.

REPEAT CHORUS

Trust yourself . . . it's alright.

Starin' at the mountain, wrestlin' with my pride.
Torn by emotion. Wantin' to move but my feet feel tied.
This indecision comes with every change.
I try to remember
a chance on myself is a certain gain.

REPEAT CHORUS

Trust yourself . . . it's alright.   (Repeat 2 times)
Somethin' tells me.

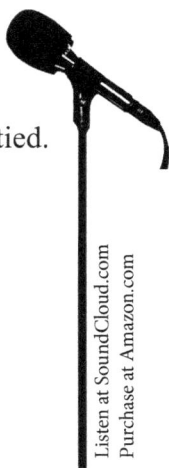

A RUMBLE DEEP INSIDE

Everyone around me had basically said,
"You stink. You suck. You don't know what you're doing"
and I accepted it... but then a little voice kept saying,
"I don't think so. I don't think it can be that bad."

— James Cameron, Filmmaker

A dream is a desire that won't be ignored. It growls from your gut like an empty stomach begging for food. Just as we need food to eat and air to breathe, dreams keep our spirit alive. It's easy to become so enchanted by the callings of the world that we ignore the callings of our heart. Olympic Gold Medal Gymnast Mary Lou Retton recognized that "each one of us has a fire in our heart for something. It's our goal in life to find it and to keep it." What dream is growling from your gut crying out for your attention? Listen for the call.

EVERYONE HAS A DREAM
A dream is born... excitement builds... we begin to move... then fear and doubt creep in. These emotions cause most of us to turn away from our dreams. Not every dream needs to be pursued but some dreams never stop calling. You may possess a passion for something that has never crossed another person's mind. Your dreams are uniquely yours. So dance, sing, open a business, go to medical school, help others in need, whatever it is. Do what moves you... despite the fear and doubt!

RECIPE FOR SUCCESS
At the age of 20, Debbi Fields a young housewife had a dream, a recipe and not much else. She wanted to open a chocolate chip cookie store. One critic knocked her idea insisting that "A cookie store is a bad idea...market research reports say America likes crispy cookies, not soft and chewy cookies like you make." Mrs. Fields ignored this criticism and built a $450 million company.[1] It takes courage to go after a dream. Your belief in yourself and your dream is more important that the opinion of others.

ONE DREAM MAY TRUMP ANOTHER

Though you may have many dreams, some dreams will take priority over others. Your dream to own a home may require you to work overtime to make more money. This may not leave you with extra time for a different dream. Your dream to have a family may put limits on your other options. Therefore, one dream may need to be completed before another can be pursued.

GULLIBLE DREAMERS

Pursuing a difficult dream is work. You will be forced to take risks, face fears and make sacrifices. A realistic plan is essential. Inspiration and talent will only get you so far. There is no easy way out and nobody can do it for you. You'll need to work to bring your dreams to reality. Don't be a gullible dreamer.

EXPIRATION DATE

Does your dream come with an expiration date? Women understand the pressure that their "biological clock" puts on a dream of having children. Athletes know that they have a limited time to make their mark in their given sport before time catches up with them. Be careful, con artists will use the fear of losing out on a great opportunity to pressure people into taking action without thinking things through.

The next time you get a "wake up call" from your dream... don't hit the snooze button.

THE LIST OF IMPOSSIBLES

As I mentioned in the introduction to this book, when I was younger, I developed some problems with my eyesight. Doctors were concerned that these problems could possibly lead to the loss of my vision. This forced me to think differently about my life. I made a list of things I wanted to do and places I wanted to see before losing my sight. In making this List of Dreams I encountered a problem. I found myself struggling to add certain things to the list, because I believed they were impossible. It was at this time that I discovered I had already, unconsciously, written another list... my "List of Impossibles."

As a child, dreams have no limits. Nothing is impossible. We can be and do anything we imagine. As we grow we are told, "Boys can't do this" or "Girls can't be that." This is the beginning of our List of Impossibles. We add to this list anytime we are convinced we cannot do something or be something that was once a dream.

When we pursue a dream and are unsuccessful, we often give up and add it to our list. Fed by self doubt, and often the pressure of others, our List of Impossibles grows longer and longer. We can become afraid to dream, because it hurts too much to think we might have to add another dream to this list.

As I reviewed my List of Impossibles, I realized there were many things on the list that I had convinced myself, or others convinced me, I couldn't do without even trying. I decided to pursue some of my smaller dreams. This gave me the skills and the confidence I needed to go after bigger challenges. My List of Impossibles began to shrink. Now I realized I had an eraser.

One thing I had convinced myself I couldn't do was draw. I had never seriously tried, so I decided to give it a shot. I looked for things to draw, but until I found a subject matter that interested me, I only made half-hearted attempts and again felt unsuccessful. At the time, I was studying Kung Fu and was excited about the beauty of the art so I decided to sketch some of the poses that interested me. I felt more satisfied with my results, but struggled when it came to recreating the details of a face. So I drew a lot of headless people for a while! When I realized I had convinced myself that I "couldn't draw faces," I also realized that I had added another item to my List of Impossibles. This drove me to look through magazines for interesting faces to draw, and give it a shot. I'm no Picasso, but I mention this to illustrate a point. I had talked myself out of so many dreams before I had ever really tried.

Use the space below or a notebook to explore your dreams. Include both your List of Dreams and your List of Impossibles.

LIST OF DREAMS:	LIST OF IMPOSSIBLES:
_____	_____
_____	_____
_____	_____
_____	_____
_____	_____
_____	_____

Rate Your Rumble
with the Passion-meter

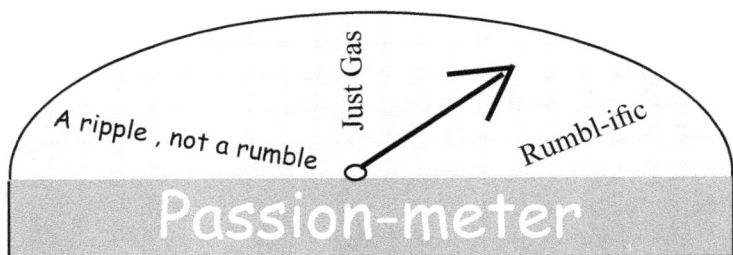

Just Gas

A ripple, not a rumble

Rumbl-ific

Passion-meter

Only passions, great passions,
can elevate the soul to great things.

– Denis Diderot,
philosopher, art critic and writer

How do you know if the rumble you feel deep inside is a dream calling… or just gas? When prompted by your gut to pursue a particular dream, your first step is to interpret what your gut is telling you by defining your dream. For example: several people may share a dream about singing. One person may want to do it professionally on a local level, another may seek a career on Broadway, while yet another may be satisfied in taking a few lessons and being a better shower-singer. All are goals about singing yet they vary in scope and therefore involve different levels of commitment, challenge, ability and risk.

Once you have defined your dream it's time to rate your rumble. The following questions will help you to rate the intensity of the passion you feel toward a particular dream. Your answers to these questions will give you a clue as to how important this dream is to you. Ultimately, only you can determine if the rumble you feel deep inside is worth pursuing.

Rate Your Rumble For This Particular Dream

(1) Define your dream as a specific, measurable goal.

(2) On a scale of 1 to 10, how passionate are you about this dream? Why do you want to pursue this dream?

(3) How long have you felt this rumble? (days, weeks, months, years). A desire that is just a passing fancy will soon stop rumbling, but a dream that rumbles a long time is more important to you.

(4) How often do you hear the rumble of this dream? You might say something like, "It's all I can think about" or "When I see others living their dream I get a strange feeling in my gut" or "I think about it every year on my birthday." Your statement is an indication of what this particular dream means to you.

(5) How loud is the rumble? You might say, "It drowns out the rest of my life" or "I can hear it calling from my heart" or "When I slow down and listen, it's there." Throughout our lives we will receive many callings from our heart. How important is this particular dream?

(6) What is the rumble in your gut telling you about this dream? You might say, "I know in my heart that I'm supposed to do this" or "It is a feeling that doesn't go away" or "I've tried to ignore it but this dream keeps calling to me."

(7) Does the rumble associated with this particular dreams rate high enough on the Passion-meter to warrant its pursuit?

None of us will ever accomplish
anything excellent or commanding
except when he listens to this whisper
which is heard by him alone.

— Ralph Waldo Emerson,
essayist, philosopher and poet

Listen
to the
whisper

Committment Calculator

Pursuing a dream is like committing to a relationship. At first it's new and exciting. But once the newness wears off and the fireworks fade, you must decide if you want the relationship to grow deeper. This takes work and commitment. It's hard for many people to commit to a relationship. The same is true about committing to a difficult dream. Dreams and relationships require time, dedication, risk, vulnerability, personal growth and sacrifice. Neither dreams nor relationships are guaranteed to work out. You must decide how dedicated you are to this particular dream. Are you committed enough to see it through?

Below are some statements that will test your commitment to this dream. Check those commitments that you are willing to make. If you have difficulty committing to this dream, pick another dream or adjust the scope of this one. For example, singing on Broadway may be changed to singing in a choir.

- ☐ I will give this dream a place of priority in my life.
- ☐ I will take my goals seriously.
- ☐ I will commit sufficient time and resources to my dream.
- ☐ I will educate myself about how to be successful and seek out qualified people for guidance.
- ☐ I will make a plan to optimize my chances for success and will revise a plan that is not working.
- ☐ When low on money, time or motivation, I will implement a plan to replenish these resources.
- ☐ I will assess and manage the risks associated with this dream, take healthy calculated risks and continually seek ways to better my odds for success.
- ☐ I will remain true to myself and my values.
- ☐ I will learn from my mistakes.
- ☐ I refuse to give up when times get tough.

- ☐ I will work through any obstacles that stand in my way.
- ☐ I will resist distractions and remove temptations that could negatively impact this dream.
- ☐ I will adapt, change and grow for the sake of this dream.
- ☐ I will make sacrifices and lifestyle changes, when needed, to get what I want.
- ☐ I will learn to manage my emotions and stress so that neither keeps me from this dream.
- ☐ I will assess my strengths and weaknesses and work on any weaknesses that hinder my efforts.
- ☐ I refuse to let critical people or my own negativity rob me of this dream.
- ☐ I will measure and reward my progress toward this dream on a regular basis.

- ☐ I acknowledge that I have chosen to pursue a difficult dream and accept that some difficult dreams don't come true. I will strive to maintain healthy balance in my life, even if it means putting some dreams on hold for the sake of my overall well-being.

X _____
(Sign Here)

Interest

There's a difference between
interest and commitment.
If you're interested in doing something,
you do it only when circumstances permit.
When you're committed to something,
you accept no excuses, just results.

— Art Turock,
motivational speaker and author

Commitment

Turning Your Dream Into A Business

If you have the desire to make a living from your dream, your dream has just become a business. Therefore, you must be prepared to handle all the challenges associated with owning a business. You don't need a Masters Degree in Business Administration but you must have a solid, viable plan. It's not enough to have the passion of an entrepreneur; you must have the skills, temperament, resources and dedication to be successful. Here are some organizations that can help.

U.S. Small Business Administration (SBA)
409 Third Street SW, Sixth Floor Washington, DC 20416
Phone: 800-827-5722 or 202-205-6673 Website: www.sba.gov.
Description: The U.S. Small Business Administration helps people start, build and grow businesses by providing four primary areas of assistance to American Small Businesses. These are: Advocacy, Management, Procurement, and Financial Assistance.

>**Office of Women's Business Ownership** (Div. of SBA)
>Description: The Office of Women's Business Ownership collaborates with many organizations to make the best possible resources available to women entrepreneurs.

>**Office of Veterans Business Development** (Div. of SBA)
>Description: The mission of the Office of Veterans Business Development is to maximize the availability, applicability and usability of all SBA small business programs for Veterans, Service-Disabled Veterans, Reserve Component Members, and their dependents or survivors.

Minority Business Development Agency (MBDA)
1401 Constitution Avenue, NW, Washington, DC 20230
Phone: 888-324-1551 Website: www.mbda.gov
Description: The Minority Business Development Agency at the U.S. Department of Commerce is the only federal agency dedicated to advancing the establishment and growth of minority-owned firms

in the United States. Through a network of minority business centers and strategic partners, MBDA works with minority entrepreneurs who wish to grow their businesses in size, scale and capacity. These firms are then better positioned to create jobs, impact local economies and expand into national and global markets. MBDA has spent more than four decades increasing the competitiveness of minority firms.

Service Corps of Retired Executives (SCORE)
Website: www.score.org.
Description: The Service Corps of Retired Executives is a nonprofit organization consisting of over 11,000 volunteers (working and/or retired business owners, executives and corporate leaders) providing free and confidential small business advice to entrepreneurs. The SCORE website has a searchable database of mentors. Simply email your questions to the mentor of your choice. Free online workshops are also available.

U.S. Chamber of Commerce
1615 H Street NW, Washington, DC 20062-2000
Website: www.uschamber.com
Description: The U.S. Chamber of Commerce is the world's largest business federation representing 3 million businesses of all sizes, sectors, and regions, as well as state and local chambers and industry associations. More than 96% of U.S. Chamber members are small businesses with 100 employees or fewer. The U.S. Chamber Small Business Nation is a community that was founded on the open exchange of information and ideas, while creating the opportunity for small businesses to speak with a unified voice.

Quit now, you'll never make it.
If you disregard this advice,
You'll be halfway there.

– David Zucker,
movie director

Quit!
You'll
Never
make it.

Know more
than people think you know.

Do more
than you are expected to do.

Seek more
than what is being offered.

Expand
beyond the imposing limits.

Soar like an eagle
as high as a star.

—LDH

IT'S YOUR LIFE

LDH

Take pride in being yourself...
It's the only thing that comes natural in a world
where being "normal" is so important.

— LDH

TELL ME WHAT LIFE'S ABOUT

This crazy world makes no sense to me.
I don't know what to believe, makes no, no sense to me.
All of my life, I've never found a reason…

Why we turn away from the precious dreams of yesterday;
never taking time to live our lives our way.

CHORUS:
Wish someone would tell me what life's about.
Searchin' everyday I come up empty.
Wish someone would tell me what life's about;
standing at the gate to a world of plenty.
I don't know, I don't know, why we live this way.
I don't know, I don't know, if we'll ever change.
I don't know, I don't know, why we live this way.
Wish someone would tell me (what life's about.)

I know this world won't look out for me.
It's my job, since I am free,
to choose my destiny.
But all of my life I've never found a reason . . .

Why we pass control.
Give away our lives, our very souls.
Then we wonder why
this way of life takes its toll.

REPEAT CHORUS

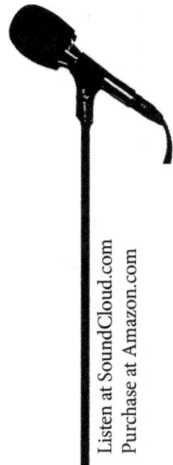

Lookin' around I see lonely faces;
troubled and down, hopin' for changes,
searchin' for a better way to live.

REPEAT CHORUS

RAGING TIGER
BEHIND PAPER BARS

A one, two, three... I was born with a dream
and it's countin' on me, yeah me, to set it free… ohhh
I know it will be a fight
to bring this dream to life
but like a tiger. . . I'm ready to fight!

A raging tiger behind paper bars
soon escapes to conquer all.
The timid mouse stays in the cage,
'cause he's afraid to fall.
I know it will be a fight
to bring this dream to life
but like a tiger. . . I'm ready to fight!

If you're like me, you were born with a dream
It may be locked inside you, but you hold the key.
I know it will be a fight
to bring this dream to life
but like a tiger. . . Get ready to fight!

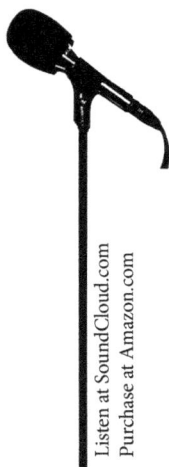

A raging tiger behind paper bars
soon escapes to conquer all.
The timid mouse stays in the cage,
'cause he's afraid to fall.
I know it will be a fight
to bring this dream to life
but like a tiger. . . Get ready to fight!

I know it will be a fight
to bring this dream to life
but like a tiger. . . Get ready to fight!

It's Your Life

If no one ever took risks,
Michelangelo would have painted
the Sistine floor.

— Neil Simon, playwright

Your dreams are yours and yours alone. If you are making all kinds of excuses about why you are not pursuing a particular dream, then that particular dream must not mean that much to you. Find one that does. We often create drama to keep ourselves too busy or too broke to do what we say we would do, if we weren't so busy or broke. It's time to check your excuses at the door and find a dream that means something to you. A dream doesn't have to take over your life. It can be as simple as trying a new hobby, taking a class or going somewhere you have always wanted to go. Do it for you.

PLAY VERSUS WORK

A big obstacle we face when beginning an exercise program is found in the term "workout." Many people see the word "work" and don't want any part of it. On the other hand, other people play tennis, play basketball and go dancing. All are great forms of exercise; and who wouldn't rather play than work? The same goes for pursuing a dream. If you find something that you love to do, something that you're passionate about, you'll see the "play" in it and accept the "work."

WHAT DO I HAVE TO LOSE?

Some risks are healthy, some are not. Ask yourself, "What do I have to lose if I give this dream a try?" Many times, we have little or nothing to lose and everything to gain. Other dreams can be quite risky. Before pursuing a dream it's a good idea to compare the risks to the rewards then decide if following this dream is a healthy pursuit. You can always redefine your dream to be fulfilling yet less risky. Take time to think about the consequences of your actions and avoid making big decisions or taking big risks when you are tired, feeling pressured or experiencing an emotional high or low. Yes, it's exciting to hear about extreme gambles that paid off, but the truth of the matter is: most long shots fall short of the mark.

A NO-RISK SITUATION

We often accept failure before we even get started because it provides the security of a no-risk situation. Attempts at success entail risk, insecurity, and often pain. But these attempts, no matter the outcome, bring self respect. While we may be able to minimize some of the risk associated with a difficult dream we usually can not eliminate it completely.

HAUNTED BY WANTS

Sooner or later you have to stop talking about what you want and take action. "Wishing for it" instead of "working at it" is like fishing without bait. We often make our lives miserable wishing things were better, yet do nothing to make them better. If you want something go after it. Even if you don't get it, you'll at least respect yourself for trying.

FREE TO BE ME

Probably the most important dream we all share is the desire to discover and become our genuine self. Often we are reluctant to be who we truly are because we are concerned about what others might

---

EGG-SCUSES

Many of us resist pursuing a dream by belching out a big "but." "But what if I fail... But I don't know how to do it... But people might laugh.... But it's too hard." We sit on our excuses like protective mother hens nurturing them instead of our dreams. Keep in mind: if you lead with your "but" you're moving backwards... and the more power you give to your excuses the bigger your "but" will grow.

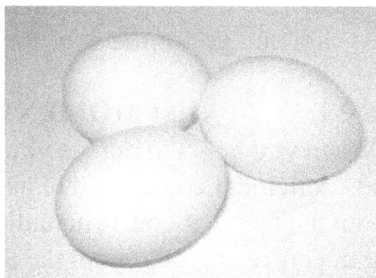

think. Our society pressures us to conform to its latest definition of "cool." It's easy to feel like a chameleon — continuously changing colors to fit into our ever changing environment. Be careful not to lose yourself in the process. When we truly accept ourselves we become less concerned about what others think and more commited to doing the work necessary to be ourselves. Find security within yourself, follow your dreams and celebrate your uniqueness.

LET YOUR DREAM BE YOUR LEGACY

In 1888, a French newspaper printed an obituary announcing the death of Dr. Alfred Nobel. It described Nobel, the inventor of dynamite, as "a merchant of death... who became rich by finding ways to kill more people faster than ever before."[1] This description of Nobel was shocking enough, but what was even more shocking was the fact that Nobel wasn't dead. The author was mistaken. When you think about it, what an opportunity this created. Nobel had a chance to see the legacy he would leave. Did you even know he invented dynamite? Be remembered as a person who dared to dream.

A CHAMPION WANTS THE BALL

Michael Jordon is a legend in the sport of basketball, a true champion. On the court he thrived under pressure. At critical times in the game, he'd call for the ball, take charge and carry the team on his back. As fans we remember the buzzer-beating shots but choose to forget the misses. You are the champion of your dream. You have no chance of winning if you don't try. So call for the ball, take your best shot and go for the win. Remember a champion wants the ball.

SWEATY-PALM MOMENTS

When you begin to pursue your dream you will realize that anxiety and excitement come hand in hand. On the one hand, you're excited about the fact that you're actually pursuing your dream. On the other hand, you're anxious about the fact that you're pursuing your dream. It's helpful to think back to other "sweaty-palm moments" like your first kiss or learning to ride a bicycle. When you focused on the reward, you were willing to take the risk. Pursuing your dream is no different. So take a deep breath, plan your path, pucker up and kiss those fears goodbye.

How Do You Define Success?

We all have the right to define success by our own standards. We are not obligated to accept anyone else's definition. The way we view success is a reflection of our values, goals, interests, self esteem and expectations. A definition of success that is empowering for one person may be stifling for another. A teenager's definition is likely to be vastly different from that of a senior citizen. Our definitions grow and change as we grow and change. Take some time to think about what is important to you. The following table will help you get started. Add your own words, if you wish. In the pursuit of your dreams you will be forced to make decisions that require you to know who you are, where you stand and what you value. What good is it to reach your dreams, if you lose yourself in the process?

What's Important To You

Check those
that apply.

_ Acceptance
_ Achievement
_ Admiration
_ Adventure
_ Affiliation
_ Approval
_ Autonomy
_ Balance
_ Be my own boss
_ Be myself
_ Commitment
_ Competence
_ Competition
_ Consistency
_ Control
_ Creativity

_ Education
_ Excitement
_ Exploration
_ Fairness
_ Faith
_ Fame
_ Family
_ Fitness
_ Flexibility
_ Free Time
_ Freedom
_ Friendship
_ Fulfillment
_ Fun
_ Getting ahead
_ Giving
_ Growth
_ Happiness
_ Health

_ Helping others
_ Honesty
_ Honor
_ Humility
_ Independence
_ Inner peace
_ Intimacy
_ Justice
_ Kindness
_ Leadership
_ Legacy
_ Leisure Time
_ Love
_ Marriage
_ Mental simulation
_ Mission
_ Passion
_ Patriotism
_ Peace of mind

_ Popularity
_ Possessions
_ Power
_ Prestige
_ Professionalism
_ Progress
_ Prosperity
_ Recognition
_ Relationships
_ Reliability
_ Respect
_ Reward
_ Risk taking
_ Roots
_ Routine

_ Security
_ Satisfaction
_ Self actualization
_ Self esteem
_ Self expression
_ Self respect
_ Self sufficiency
_ Sense of purpose
_ Serenity
_ Service
_ Single life
_ Spirituality
_ Stability
_ Status
_ Stimulation

_ Structure
_ Success
_ Tradition
_ Travel
_ Trust
_ Truth
_ Values
_ Variety
_ Wealth
_ Wholeness
_ Wisdom

PRIORITIZE YOUR VALUES

From the previous table select
your Top 5 Values and list them below.

1. _____   4. _____

2. _____   5. _____

3. _____

*It's not hard to make decisions
when you know what your values are.*

— Roy Disney

GUESS WHAT THEY HAVE IN COMMON

It's easy to fall into the trap of thinking that people who are living their dreams must have had it easier than the rest of us. Here are some examples of people who refused to let anything interfere with their dream. Can you guess what they have in common?

Dr. Ruth Westheimer (psychologist, author), Eddie Murphy (comedian, actor), Dan O'Brien (Olympic decathlete), Marilyn Monroe (actress), Dr. Wayne Dyer (author, motivational speaker), Tom Monaghan (founder of Domino's Pizza) and Allison Anders (independent film director)[2]

— Foster Kids

Thomas Edison (inventor), Marlee Matlin (Academy Award winning actress), Cliff Bastin (British footballer), Bernard Bragg (actor, director, playwright and lecturer), Guillaume Amontons (inventor and physicist), Francisco Goya (painter), Terrylene Sachetti (actress, poet, storyteller, mime, and dancer) and Heather Whitestone McCallum (Miss America)[3]

— Hearing Impaired

Richard Branson (founder of Virgin Brand), John Chambers (CEO of Cisco), Ingvar Kamprad (founder of IKEA), Jay Leno (comedian, TV host), Charles Schwab (founder of U.S. brokerage firm), Leonardo da Vinci (renaissance man), Stephen J. Cannell (TV producer, writer, actor), Paul Orfalea (founder of Kinko's), Jackie Stewart (race car driver), Dr. Jack R. Horner (paleontologist), Henry Winkler (actor, director, producer), Erin Brockovich (legal clerk) and Winston Churchill (politician)[4]
Note: According to a study by Julie Logan, professor of entrepreneurship at the Cass Business School in London, 35% of U.S. entrepreneurs have this condition.[5]

— Dyslexia

Kenny G (saxophonist), Tom Dolan (world record holding swimmer), Jackie Joyner-Kersee (track and field), Art Monk (football), Alice Cooper (rock musician, performer), Elias James Corey (Nobel Prize winner for chemistry), Bruce Davidson (equestrian champion), Bill Koch (cross-country skier), Greg Louganis (diving champion), Maclyn McCarty (biologist), George Murray (wheelchair marathon champion), Martin Scorsese (film director), Karin Smith (Olympic javelin specialist), Paul Sorvino[6] (operatic tenor, actor) and Robert Joffrey[7] (Joffrey ballet company)

—Asthma

Dan Ackroyd (comedian, actor), Jim Eisenreich (baseball), Tim Howard (soccer goal keeper), Howard Hughes (industrialist), Michael Wolff[8] (jazz pianist, composer, actor), Jeremy "Twitch" Stenberg (Freestyle Motocross champion)[9] and Brad Cohen (Teacher of the Year)[10]

— Tourette's Syndrome

Christy Brown (author, painter and poet), Geri Jewell (comedian, actress), Stephen Hawking (physicist), Josh Blue[11] (comedian), Bill Porter[12] (top selling door-to-door salesman), David Ring[13] (evangelist) and Abbey Curran (Miss Iowa).[14]

— Cerebral Palsy

Carlos Santana[15] (musician), Laveranues Coles[16] (football), Oprah Winfrey[17] (TV host), Teri Hatcher[18] (actress), Tori Amos[19] (songwriter), Joyce Meyer[20] (evangelist) and Mary J. Blige (singer)[21]

— Survived sexual abuse

Bo Diddley (performer), Dave Thomas (founder of Wendy's), D.M.C. (hip hop artist), Faith Hill (singer), Tim McGraw (singer), John Lennon (musician), Dan O'Brien (decathlete), Lynnette

Cole (Miss USA), Nancy Reagan (First Lady), Edward Albee (Pulitzer Prize winning playwright), Art Linkletter (radio and TV personality) and Steve Jobs (co-founder of Apple computer)[22]

— Adopted

Aretha Franklin (entertainer), Halle Berry (actress), "Smokin' Joe" Frazier (boxer), Nicole Johnson (Miss America), Nick Jonas (singer/songwriter, actor), Walt Kelly (animator, cartoonist), Billie Jean King (tennis), Winnie Mandela (anti-apartheid leader) and Scott Verplank (golfer)[23]

— Diabetes

Rosario Dawson (actress, singer), Chad Michael Murray (actor, model, spokesperson), Tyra Banks (TV personality, model), Pierce Brosnan[24] (actor), Tom Cruise (actor), Mel Gibson (actor), Harrison Ford (actor), Michelle Pfeiffer[25] (actress), Christina Aguilera (singer/songwriter), Steven Spielberg (film director), Chris Rock (comedian), Eva Longoria (actress), and Tiger Woods (golfer)[26]

— Endured Bullying

Wilma Rudolph (track and field gold medalist), Eleanor Abbott (inventor of the game "Candy Land"), Francis Ford Coppola (filmmaker, producer, screenwriter), Pete Dawkins (Heisman Trophy winner, Rhodes Scholar, U.S. Army Brigadier General), Garth Drabinsky (theatrical producer), Margarete Steiff (toymaker), Owen Roizman (cinematographer), James DePreist (conductor), David Sanborn (jazz saxophonist), Allen B. DuMont (scientist, inventor, and television pioneer), Elsie MacGill (first female aircraft designer), Fred Lawrence Whipple (astronomer) and Wah Chang (film prop artist)[27]

— Polio

James Earl Jones (the voice of Darth Vader), Joseph R. Biden Jr. (Vice President of the United States), John Stossel (journalist), Bill Walton (basketball, sportscaster), Bruce Willis (actor, singer), Carly Simon (singer/songwriter), Julia Roberts (actress, model), Nicholas Brendon (actor), Rowan Atkinson (comedian, writer, actor) and Bill Withers (singer-songwriter)[28]

— Stuttering

Ty Pennington (carpenter, TV personality), Michael Phelps (swimmer), Howie Mandell (comedian, TV host), James Carville[29] (political consultant), Terry Bradshaw (football, actor), Glenn Beck (political commentator), Paul Orfalea (founder of Kinko's), Robert Toth (sculptor) and Peter Wright (attorney)[30]

— Attention Deficit Hyperactivity Disorder

Bob Vila (home improvement TV Host), David Thomas (founder of Wendy's), Bob Schieffer (TV Journalist), Harold Prince (Broadway producer), F. Lee Bailey (attorney), Gloria Steinem (publisher of MS. Magazine), Stanley Sporkin (federal judge), Denise Austin (fitness expert) and Buddy Hackett (comedian)[31]

— Overcame Shyness

The only disability in life is a bad attitude.

— Scott Hamilton,
ice skater

Even when the
candles on your cake
become a
fire hazard...

It's never
too late
to dream

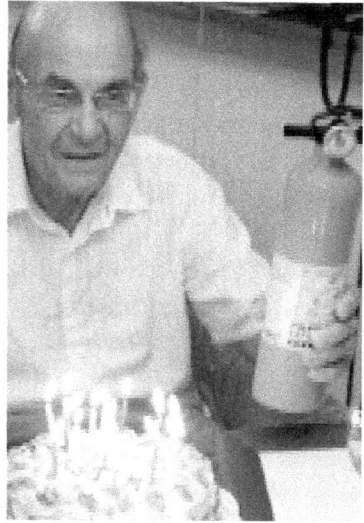

It's easy to discount ourselves and our dreams with statements like, "I'm too old" or "I don't have any talent." Don't sell yourself short. A man in his fifties whose dream is to become a professional football player has probably missed his shot. He could modify this dream to one in which he is involved in football in a way that brings him satisfaction.

Make a list of things you've always wanted to do. Pick one, make a plan and do it. Here are some examples of people who defied their age and dared to dream.

- At 41, swimmer Dara Torres competed in her fifth Olympics and won three Silver Medals.[32] At 42, Rodney Dangerfield began his career in comedy.[33] At 45, George Foreman recaptured the Boxing Heavyweight Title[34] and Mary Kay Ash began building her cosmetics empire.[35]

- At 58, James "Doc" Councilman became the oldest man to swim the English Channel.[36]

- At 60, Clara Barton founded the American Red Cross.[37] At 64, Francis Chichester sailed solo around the world.[38] At 66, Colonel Sanders established Kentucky Fried Chicken.[39]

- At 70, Paul Newman became the oldest winner of a NASCAR auto race by winning the Daytona 24-hour Sports Car Endurance Race.[40] At 76, Grandma Moses started painting when arthritis pain forced her to give up needlework.[41] At 77, John Glen became the oldest person to go into outer space.[42]

- At 80, years and 292 days old Jessica Tandy won an Oscar for "Driving Miss Daisy."[43] At 87, Mary Baker Eddy started The Christian Science Monitor.[44]

- At 95, Nola (Hill) Ochs became the world's oldest college graduate earning her diploma from Fort Hays State University.[45]

- At 102, Elsie McLean became the oldest golfer ever to make a hole-in-one on a regulation course. She had been playing golf for 80 years and this was her first ace.[46]

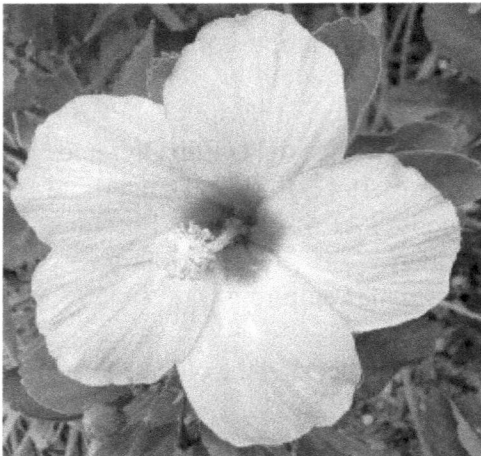

And the day came
when the risk
to remain tight
in a bud
was more painful
than the risk
it took
to blossom.

— Anais Nin, diarist

A CLAIM TO BLAME

When you focus on your limitations that's all you see. So stop trading your claim to fame for a claim to blame and discover your dreams. When you've been through enough hell, you'll realize that you are responsible for creating your own sense of heaven.

- ◆ Even after he went deaf, Beethoven's passion for composing would not be squelched. He still found a way to compose his 9th symphony.[47] Thomas Edison considered his hearing problems to be a blessing because it enabled him to focus more effectively and not be distracted.[48]

- ◆ Even after losing his arm in the Civil War, John Wesley Powell wanted to pursue his lifelong dream of being an explorer. His father discouraged him saying, "Wes, you are a maimed man, get this notion of science and adventure out of your mind." Powell ignored this advice and, in 1869, led expeditions down the Colorado River to explore the Grand Canyon.[49]

- ◆ Shaun White was born with a congenital heart defect. He underwent two heart surgeries before the age of five. This would cause most of us to give up on a career in extreme sports but Shaun is a champion in both professional snowboarding and skateboarding.[50]

Time won't wait until we find
the perfect time to bring a dream to life.
Time can't give us back the minutes
we were waiting for . . . the perfect time.

— LDH

UNDERSTAND YOUR MOTIVATION

Everyone has the potential to succeed at whatever he or she chooses; but potential is not the biggest factor... perseverance is. The drive to develop your potential is the determining factor of success. What is the driving force that is pushing your toward your dream? Look over the following list to get an understanding of your motivation. Pick one dream and select those words that apply. Add to the list, if you wish.

WHAT MOVES YOU?

Check those that apply.

	_ Control	_ Health
	_ Creativity	_ Helping others
	_ Criticism	_ Honor
_ A better life	_ Curiosity	_ Hunger
_ Acceptance	_ Deadlines	_ Independence
_ Achievement	_ Desire	_ Inner peace
_ Adventure	_ Destiny	_ Innovation
_ Affiliation	_ Discovery	_ Inspiration
_ Anger	_ Dissatisfaction	_ Interest
_ Anxiety reduction	_ Duty	_ Intimacy
_ Appreciation	_ Enjoyment	_ Jealousy
_ Approval	_ Entertainment	_ Joy
_ Authenticity	_ Excitement	_ Justice
_ Autonomy	_ Exploration	_ Leadership
_ Be my own boss	_ Faith	_ Leave a legacy
_ Be myself	_ Fame	_ Love
_ Bills to pay	_ Family	_ Lust
_ Camaraderie	_ Fear	_ Meaning to life
_ Challenge	_ Financial freedom	_ Mental stimulation
_ Change	_ Fitness	_ Mission
_ Commitment	_ Freedom	_ Money
_ Compassion	_ Fulfillment	_ Need
_ Compensation	_ Fun	_ Novelty
_ Competition	_ Growth	_ Opportunity
_ Concern	_ Happiness	_ Order

_ Passion _ Recognition _ Sense of purpose
_ Patriotism _ Responsibility _ Spirituality
_ Payoff _ Revenge _ Stability
_ Peace of mind _ Reward _ Status
_ Peer pressure _ Risk _ Stimulation ·
_ Pleasure _ Routine _ Stress
_ Popularity _ Satisfaction _ Success
_ Power _ Security _ Survival
_ Prestige _ Self actualization _ Tradition
_ Pride _ Self esteem _ Truth
_ Promotion _ Self expression _ Values
_ Prosperity _ Self respect _ Wealth
_ Purpose _ Self sufficiency _ Wholeness
_ Rebellion _ Sense of belonging

PRIORITIZE YOUR MOTIVATORS

From the previous table select
your Top 5 Motivators for this dream and list them below.

1. _____

2. _____

3. _____

4. _____

5. _____

Give me a stock clerk with a goal
and I'll give you a man who will make history.
Give me a man with no goals
and I'll give you a stock clerk.

— J.C. Penney,
entrepreneur

Known For Success
But Motivated By Failure

- Every cartoon Charles Schultz submitted for his high school yearbook was rejected by the yearbook staff.[51]

- Babe Ruth hit 714 home runs, but struck out 1,330 times.[52]

- Basketball legend Michael Jordan was cut from his high school basketball team as a sophomore.[53] Boston Celtics star Bob Cousy was cut twice.[54]

- Matt Lauer was fired 5 times in 5 years before getting the Today Show position.[55]

- R.H. Macy's first four retail dry goods stores failed.[56]

An inventor fails 999 times,
and if he succeeds once, he's in.
He treats his failures
simply as practice shots.

— Charles F. Kettering, inventor
(He received more than 300 patents.)

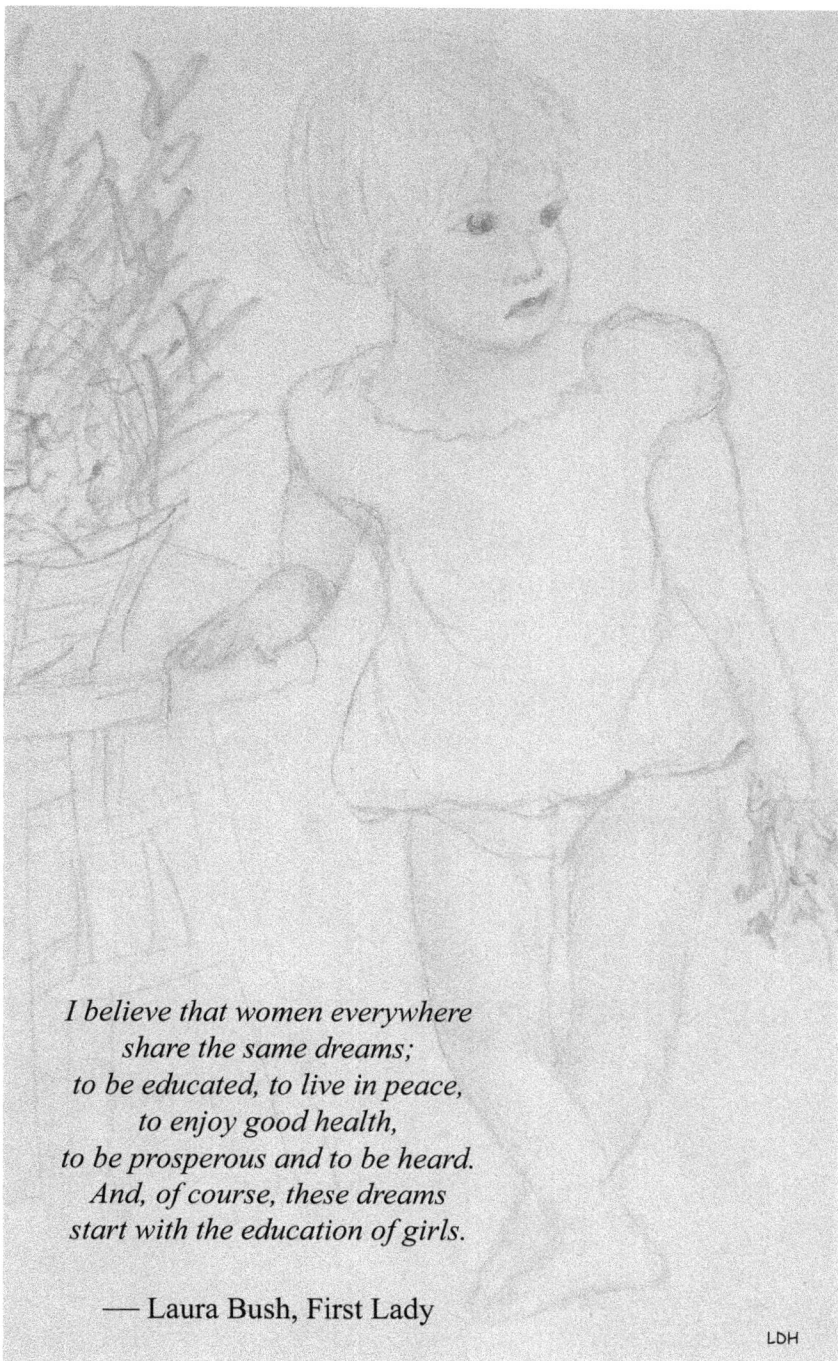

*I believe that women everywhere
share the same dreams;
to be educated, to live in peace,
to enjoy good health,
to be prosperous and to be heard.
And, of course, these dreams
start with the education of girls.*

—— Laura Bush, First Lady

LDH

Many people equate
dreams to illusions;
but in dreams
there is hope
and hope
is the driving force
to a better world.

— LDH

THAT
FIRST
STEP

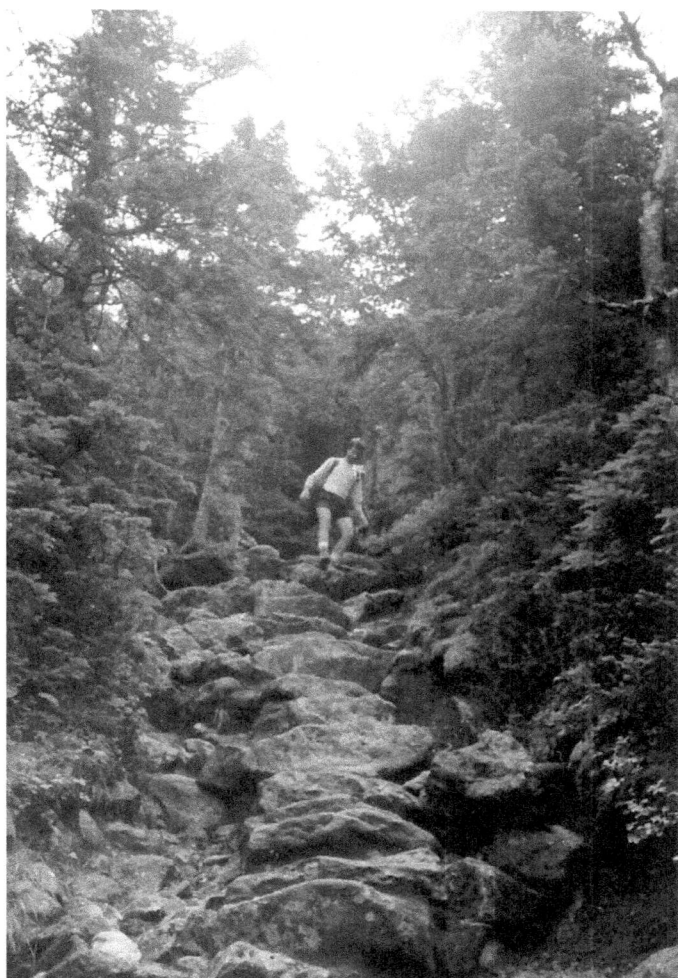

Photo: Hiking down from a stay at Lakes of The Clouds an Appalation Mountain Club Lodge on the southern shoulder of Mount Washington.

SO MANY MOUNTAINS

I was staring at the mountain top
with a dream in mind.
And as soon as the time was right
I would make the climb.
But whenever I had the time
the sky looked like rain.
I was wonderin' if I'd ever see that day.

CHORUS:
So many mountains still yet to climb.
So many dreams weigh on my mind.
So many mountains callin' my name
that it seems my life
is so many mountains away.

On the day I started up the trail
my legs were strong.
I didn't know how many times I'd stumble and fall.
But when my side ached with doubt,
I'd grit my teeth,
and shout at the summit,
"I refuse to be beat!"

REPEAT CHORUS

When I made it to the top
I didn't realize what I'd see from there.
A hundred mountain peaks sayin',
"Climb me, if you dare."

So many mountains still yet to climb.
So many dreams weigh on my mind.
So many mountains callin' my name
but now I live my life
knowin' mountains won't stand in my way.

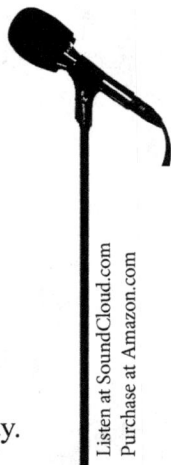

THAT FIRST STEP

The indispensable first step
to getting the things you want out of life
is this: decide what you want.

— Ben Stein,
actor, comedian, speechwriter, game
show host and commentator

To get anyplace but lost, you must first decide where you wish to go. Many people say, "I just want to be happy" but give no thought to what it is that makes them happy. First, you must decide what you want and then work through specific, measurable goals to bring these things, people and experiences into your life. Remember, the perfect plan is useless without the first step. Find your passion, decide your direction, plan your path, take the first step and never give up.

HUNT AND GATHER
Before you begin your journey you'll need to gather information about your quest. Make a list of resources that will provide useful information about your goals. Include periodicals, books, journals, DVD's, classes, workshops, organizations, public speakers, entrepreneurs and teachers.

WHAT WILL THE NEIGHBORS THINK?
We often put off taking the first step toward our dream because we are worried about what others will think. We don't want to look foolish. When you commit to a dream you are making a commitment that is bigger than your dream. You are making a commitment to be true to yourself. Pursue your dream in the way that you believe is right for you – not merely the way you think is acceptable to others. What's more foolish… taking a shot at your dream or denying that you have one?

GO IT ALONE

If you are waiting for the approval of others, or until you find a partner who shares your passion, you will probably never take a single step toward your dream. You must be willing to step out on your own. If you want something bad enough you'll do whatever it takes to get it, if you don't; you won't. It's up to you.

TIMING

Is the timing right for you to be able to give this particular dream what it requires to be successful? A mom raising a family may need to postpone one particular dream until her children are in school. A different dream may fit perfectly into her schedule. If the timing is not right, list the reasons why followed by a specific time when the timing will be better. Come back to this dream when you can give it what it needs, but remember, the timing will probably never be perfect.

MANAGEABLE STEPS

The first time I walked into a martial arts dojo and observed the black belts training, I was overwhelmed. They were doing things physically that I believed I could never do. The instructor calmly explained that these complex movements could be broken down into a

Photo: Here I am (on the left) with my brother Ted at my Martial Arts Studio.

series of simpler ones. By practicing basic movements students build a strong foundation. They can then string these movements together to create more complex patterns. When faced with a difficult dream break it down into its simpler, more manageable steps.

FEAR IS A FLASHING RED LIGHT

Fear can stop us in our tracks and keep us from taking the first step toward a dream. If you think about it, fear can actually be a good thing. It's a red light that flashes inside warning us to stop, look around, think about the next move and then proceed with caution. Just because we have fear about a dream, it doesn't mean that we should not proceed. Listen to what your fear is telling you and work to resolve the issues it

*Fear hides
amongst the trees
and waits
for the right moment
to steal away
the wealth
of a new experience.*

— LDH

MANAGE YOUR FEAR

Following the 9-11 crisis Rudy Giuliani, Mayor of New York City, was asked how he and others could cope with the new fears we share as a result of the attack. He responded, "Manage your fear. Recognize you're gonna be scared but face it and move forward." Pursuing a difficult dream will be scary at times. It will lead you to unfamiliar places, stir your emotions as well as challenge your courage and faith.

presents. When you feel fear... stop and consider what you are getting into, decide if you want to proceed despite the fear and make a plan that will move you forward as safely as possible.

TAKE A CHANCE

When I was younger I had written many poems, but was nervous about reciting them in front of a poetry group. Public speaking scared me, but everyone else in the group was doing it, so I had to give it a try. I shook and stammered my way through my poem. When done, I breathed a sigh of relief for just getting through it. After the meeting a woman approached me. She thanked me for sharing the poem and asked if we could talk. She said that the message of my poem had touched her deeply. She then asked if she could share something with me that she had never told anyone before. She went on to say that her father had just passed away, but that she didn't know whether to mourn or rejoice. He had sexually abused her, her whole life.

Six months later I bumped into her at a local pizza place and her life seemed to have completely turned around. She was now counseling teens who had similar experiences and was publishing a newsletter on the subject. This experience taught me that it's important to take a chance, even if we have to shake and stammer our way through it. We never know the impact our actions may have on others.

THE JOURNEY

It is critical that you find pleasure in the pursuit of your dreams. Putting off your happiness or contentment until you reach your goals can be a big mistake. Some dreams don't come true. Thomas Edison said he found his greatest pleasure in the work that precedes what the world calls success. Enjoy the journey.

MANY FIRST STEPS

To reach your dream you must make a decision to take a new first step day after day. Each day will bring with it another challenge leading you into unfamiliar territory. You'll need to take action toward your goal whether you feel like it or not.

GO APE ... OVER YOUR DREAMS

When I was 16, I wanted very much to have a career working with animals. A career advisor recommended taking photos of pet dogs. When the advisor found out that I planned to travel to Africa to study wildlife, she told me that it was inappropriate; that I would have no chance of doing anything like that. Everyone who knew what I wanted to do thought that I should look into more practical work. Everyone, that is, but my mother. Whatever I felt I had to try, she fully supported me.[1]

— Jane Goodall

(For 45-years Goodall studied chimpanzee social and family interactions at Gombe Stream National Park in Tanzania.)

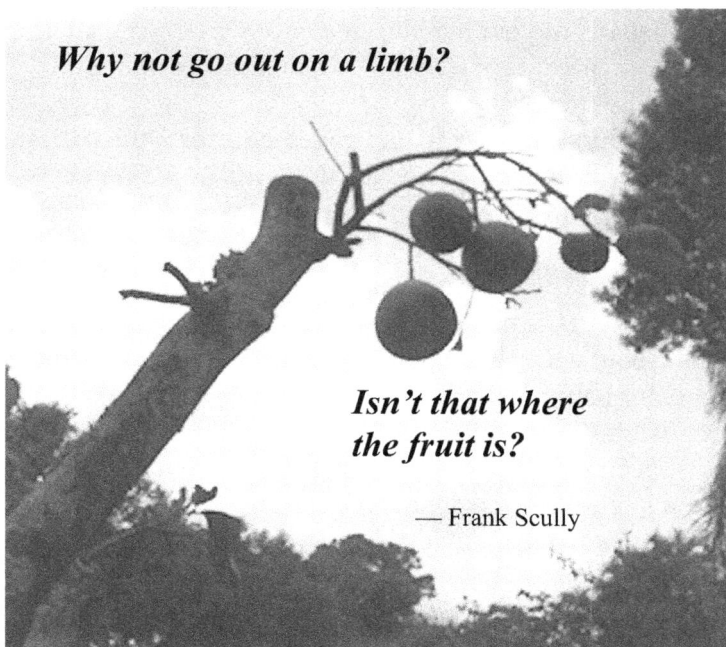

Why not go out on a limb?

Isn't that where the fruit is?

— Frank Scully

Photo: I've always dreamed of having fruit trees. This is my grapefruit tree. I also grow mangos, lemons, bananas, pineapples and more.

OUR BUBBLE
OF COMFORT

Do you find yourself doing the same thing over and over again? Not because you have to, but merely out of habit – the same routine, same foods, same hangouts, same friends, same clothes, and so on. Though we find comfort in our routine, over time it can become confining and boring. Even though we may wish to venture beyond our sphere of comfort, the fear of change often keeps us from breaking free. It's like we create our perfect world within a snow globe, a bubble of comfort, and then never step beyond it. A problem arises when our dreams lie outside of our comfort zone... and difficult dreams usually do.

If you're struggling with this dilemma, remember, a snow globe doesn't come to life until you shake things up. If your comfort zone has begun to feel more like a cage you'll need to break free. Here are some tips to help you step out of your comfort zone and toward your dreams. So break out of your bubble, creep away from your comfort zone and ease out of your easy chair. Your dreams are waiting.

1. Change anything just to get more comfortable with change. Try something new, anything new, on a regular basis. This will give you momentum to make tougher changes.
2. Ask a trusted friend to introduce you to an activity that is new to you yet familiar to your friend.
3. Think about why you want to change, what you will gain if you do change and what you will lose if you don't. Use your dreams as motivation.
4. Set a specific goal, write it down and include a deadline for completion. Remember to measure your progress and reward yourself in a way that keeps you moving forward.

BREAK OUT
OF YOUR BUBBLE

You have to leave the city of your comfort
and go into the wilderness of your intuition.
What you'll discover will be wonderful.
What you'll discover will be yourself.

– Alan Alda,
actor, director and screenwriter

THE IMPACT OF PURSUING YOUR DREAM

*Problems arise in that one has to find a balance
between what people need from you
and what you need for yourself.*

— Jessye Norman,
Opera Singer

We don't pursue our dreams in a vacuum. The demands and responsibilities of life cannot be put on hold until we reach our goals. Not only will you need to develop a plan for reaching your dream, you will need to develop a plan about how to incorporate the act of pursuing your dream into the rest of your life. How will you support yourself and your pursuit financially? How will you free up time within your schedule to devote to your dream? What impact will pursuing your dream have on your family, job, marriage, friendships, health and so on? Basic survival needs like food and shelter must be met before you proceed. One look at the tabloids and you'll see many celebrities who have reached success, yet their lives have fallen apart because they failed to seek a healthy balance. In a notebook, describe how the pursuit of your dream will impact your life. Include both positive and negative elements. Remember to describe the impact of pursuing your dream, not your life once you have attained your dream.

Consider the impact on your…

CAREER… FAMILY… FINANCES…

HEALTH… LIFESTYLE

RELATIONSHIPS…

TIME… SELF ESTEEM…

NOW consider the impact of NOT pursuing your dream!

> *Success comes in cans,*
> *not cant's.*
>
> — Unknown

> *I have it embedded in my head*
> *that I have what I need to survive and that is that.*
> *You can't focus on what you dont have*
> *because you're never gonna have it.*
>
> — Charlie Plaskon,
> Ironman Triathlete (Blind)

DISCOVER YOUR DREAMS

There is a tremendous amount of romanticism which surrounds going off on expeditions to remote parts of the world and camping in tents, and living in a desert and struggling with all of the trials and tribulations that one encounters. But, I think that what really intrigued me was the fact that I felt that this was and still is really, a science, a form of inquiry, which is still in its infancy. That there were so many things yet to be discovered, that the science itself would have, in my lifetime, still lots of surprises.[2]

— Donald Johanson,
anthropologist (Discoverer of Lucy)

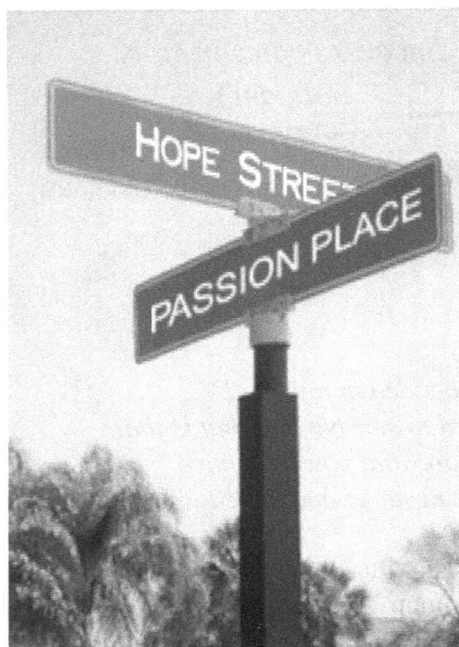

Start Here

Dreams start
at the corner
of Hope and
Passion.

Fire and Fuel

Passion is the spark
that starts your dream's engine
but commitment is the fuel
that keeps it running.

Make A Map

Be aware that even with clear directions you are likely to encounter detours, potholes and unmarked exits. Update your map as needed and keep moving forward with an eye on your goals.

Consult Your Compass

Use your values as your compass. Success lies in the direction where your goals align with your values.

Be a Pioneer Despite The Fear

- In 1638, Anne Hutchinson was banished from Massachusetts Bay Colony for preaching.[3]

- In 1822, Joseph Marion Hernandez became the first Hispanic American to serve in Congress.[4]

- In 1872, Susan B Anthony was jailed for attempting to vote.[5]

- In 1910, Alice Stebbins Wells was sworn in as the first official police woman in the United States.[6]

- In 1916, Margaret Sanger was jailed for opening a birth control clinic.[7]

- In 1926, Gertrude Caroline Ederle became the first woman to swim the English Channel.[8]

- In the mid 1940s, Rachel Carson began speaking out against industrial irresponsibility and launched a global environmental movement.[9]

- In 1947, Jackie Robinson made his first Major League Baseball appearance breaking the sport's color barrier.[10]

- In 1955, Rosa Parks refused to give up her seat in the front of a bus.[11]

- In 1967, Thurgood Marshall became the first African American to serve on the Supreme Court of the United States.[12]

- In 1973, tennis player Billie Jean King convinced her colleagues to form a union demanding equal prize money for men and women. That same year the U.S. Open complied.[13]

- In 2009, Sarah Thomas became the first woman to officiate a college football bowl game when she worked as a line judge during the Little Caesars Pizza Bowl.[14]

SOMEONE TO CLING TO

LDH

THE SPIRIT LYING DORMANT

Life went on in stride
passing like a whisper
deafened ears denied.
My dream — only to survive.

Numb to this demise,
you helped me bridge the distance
to the me inside.
For once I felt I was alive.

CHORUS:
'Cause you could see
the spirit lying dormant within me.
You took a chance and found a way
to coax my spirit from the grey.
And like a dove
the spirit lying dormant soared with love,
beyond the walls that once encaged
free to live and love and play.

How could you have known
that deep beneath my fortress
I was more than stone.
My dreams are finally free to grow.

REPEAT CHORUS

... and dream and soar
to galaxies yet to be explored.

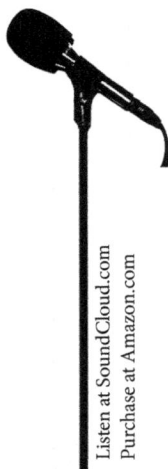

SOMEONE TO CLING TO

A friend is someone who knows the song
in your heart and can sing it back to you
when you have forgotten the words.

— Unknown

Going after a difficult dream can, at times, be disheartening. It's easy to feel isolated. Therefore, it's important to find people who can relate to what you are doing and offer support and encouragement. It's important to remember that friends and family members may believe in you, but not understand the demands of your dream. Within your support system, not only do you need people who inspire, motivate and support you, you also need people who will challenge you to do your best.

BUILD A DREAM TEAM
Your Dream Team is the support system of people who will bolster your efforts toward your dream. Many people make the mistake of filling their team with only cheerleaders. Cheerleaders are always positive, upbeat and supportive whether you are on the right track or not. They will lift your spirits but not offer much in the form of direction. That's where your coach or mentor comes in. Coaches look at the big picture. They keep you focused, prepared and accountable. A good coach will point out your weaknesses and teach you how to capitalize on your strengths. Your peers are those people who share your dream. They understand your struggles. Peers can lift each other up, share experiences and provide a soft place to fall. Now go assemble your Dream Team.

BUT IF I CHANGE
MY FRIENDS WON'T LIKE ME
People who are truly your friends will support you in your pursuit of dreams. As you grow and change, your friends have the opportunity to grow and change also; that's their choice, not yours. It's hard to

let go of friendships; but if you must give up on your dreams to keep your friends, they're not worth it. When a friend reaches out to a friend it should be to lift him up rather than hold him back. Don't be surprised if others don't share your enthusiasm for a dream. As you grow and change, your true friends will stick with you. Plus, you'll make new friends with more in common.

CARING CAN SOUND LIKE CRITICISM

It's normal for those who love you, to want the best for you. If you are attempting a dream that is risky, people who truly care about you will be concerned. They may, out of love, try to alert you to a problem with your plan. They don't want to see you get hurt. No one else can know how strongly your desire for a dream burns in your heart. That is something only you can know. Just remember, sometimes our passion for a dream blinds us to the enormity of the challenge. You can ease the concerns of others by developing a cohesive plan that minimizes your risk and maximizes your chances for success. The chapter entitled, "Getting to Your Goals" will help you develop such a plan.

A SINKING FEELING

Watch out for "yes men." These cheerleaders may be even more dangerous than critics. "Yes men" will praise your every action, providing a false sense of security that blinds you to the reality of the situation. It's important to find someone who, when asked, will be brutally honest with you. You may not always like what this person has to say, but a "yes man" will smile, wave and applaud you as your ship slowly goes under. Brutal honesty may give you a sinking feeling, but it may be just the advice you need to keep your ship afloat.

The individual has always had to struggle
to keep from being overwhelmed by the tribe.
If you try it, you will be lonely often, and sometimes frightened.
But no price is too high to pay
for the privilege of owning yourself.

— Friedrich Nietzsche, Philosopher

KEY CONTACTS:
Decision Makers and Investors

Some dreams require a connection to a key contact. A writer may need a publisher, an actor may need an agent and an entrepreneur may need an investor. Successful decision makers and investors receive many inquiries. You are just one voice in the crowd vying for their attention. You must stand out to be noticed. Once you get their attention, be professional or it's over.

You may have only one chance to impress a key contact. Make sure you are prepared. Respect the person's time. Listen carefully to the advice and don't wear out your welcome. Appearance counts. Keep your presentation short, simple and focused. Your enthusiasm will be contagious only as long as you sustain their interest; beyond that it becomes annoying. Even if your dream would be a good investment you may have to work one hundred leads to get one sale. When seeking key members of your team be careful who you pay for services. For example, an author or songwriter should not pay a publisher. The publisher will share in the profits raised by the sale of your work.

BUT I'M THE NEXT...

But I'm the next... (fill in the blank.) Says who! People in positions of power hear this everyday. To sift through the deluge of these declarations they must consider the source. You may believe you are the next Maria Carey, Maya Angelou or Cary Grant but you'll need to prove it. Don't wait for a break to develop your potential. Develop it now and make your own breaks. Create a buzz. When others with credibility speak on your behalf your stock goes way up. So earn some credits, build your resume and more doors will open for you.

WHY WON'T THEY TAKE MY CALLS?

Do you look at every piece of junk mail, read every advertisement and accept every call from telemarketers? Of course not, you have more important things to do. Your time is too valuable. If you are wondering why nobody of importance responds to your inquiries, you must realize that your inquiries are their junk mail. Decision makers must protect their time and will set up barriers or gatekeepers to perform that role. Busy people don't have the luxury of responding to every correspondence from every prospective dreamer. To the people you are trying to reach, unprofessional solicitations are a nuisance. Even if your presentation is professional; you will still need to go through the proper channels to get noticed and taken seriously.

INVESTORS

If you want people to invest in your dream you must present yourself in a way that instills confidence in the investment. People don't invest with just money. They invest their time, energy, support and emotions. Be prepared for doubters. You must be able to squelch an investor's concerns and have a solid answer for their most common question, "What's in it for me?" If a person buys into your dream it is critical that he or she doesn't feel cheated. For example, one spouse may support the other financially during the pursuit of a dream. This can become burdensome, though, if the support becomes too one-sided. If financial investors are needed, seek an evaluation of the investment from an unbiased, independent source with no emotional attachment. Family members and friends may think with their hearts and not have the skills to understand the risk.

MENTORS

Seek out people who have skills and experience that relate to your goals; preferably people who have lived your dream. A mentor will assist you in planning your direction, guide you around obstacles, introduce you to important contacts, keep you on schedule, evaluate your progress, provide encouragement and demand accountability. A good mentor will inspire you to be your best and won't hesitate to call you to the carpet when you're slacking off. Make a list of the challenges that you face with this dream. Then add the names of people who may be able to offer guidance. Refer to the section "That's What Friends Are For" for ideas.

The trick is getting noticed naturally,
without screaming or without tricks.

— Leo Burnett, advertising executive

THAT'S WHAT FRIENDS ARE FOR

*I not only use all the brains I have
but all I can borrow.*

— Woodrow Wilson, U.S. President

When pursuing a difficult dream we face a multitude of challenges. Our friends can be a great resource. We all know people with expertise or experience that we admire. Obviously, a friend who is a lawyer can assist you with legal questions, but don't overlook the attributes of your friends that may not be so obvious.

Make a list of the specific challenges that you must overcome to reach your goals. Next to each challenge write the names of people who may be able to offer assistance. Here are some examples.

The friend who is...

- **Adventurous**: can help you to be more spontaneous, to trust your gut, to take chances and to live with passion.
- **Analytical**: can review your plan and offer detailed feedback.
- **A bargain hunter**: can offer suggestions on how to save money for your dream.
- **Cool under pressure**: can teach you how to remain calm in a crisis, manage your emotions and deal with stress.
- **Creative**: can share techniques that will help you to tap into the power of your imagination and to see new perspectives with regard to common problems.
- **A successful entrepreneur**: can guide you through business-related issues.
- **Familiar with failure**: may provide important insights learned from mistakes.
- **Good with words**: can help you with correspondences and presentations.

- **Health-conscious**: can teach you how to boost your energy level through exercise and better nutrition.
- **A high achiever**: can show you how to set goals, assess risk, stay focused, juggle many projects, persevere through adversity and resist doubt.
- **Good at time management**: can share strategies that will help you make time for your dream.
- **Persistent**: can educate you about determination, resilience and willpower.
- **Open minded**: can open your eyes to when your attitudes and perspectives are limiting your thinking.
- **Successful in sales**: can teach you how to present yourself professionally and how to recover from rejection.
- **Optimistic**: can keep you positive during difficult times.
- **Organized**: can help you become more efficient through planning and organization.
- **Strong willed**: can show you how to tap into your inner strength and overcome obstacles.
- **Overcoming self defeating behaviors**: can support you in overcoming yours and share lessons learned.
- **Practical**: can bring you back to reality when you stray.
- **Resilient**: can train you how to bounce back after a defeat or adapt to change.
- **A risk taker**: can educate you about evaluating risk and maximizing your odds for success.
- **Focused**: can assist you with setting clear, measurable goals and realistic deadlines as well as how to minimize distractions.
- **Stable**: can offer instruction about maintaining a healthy balance to your life.
- **Strong in faith**: can keep you believing when you want to quit.
- **A technical wizard**: can guide you through technical problems.

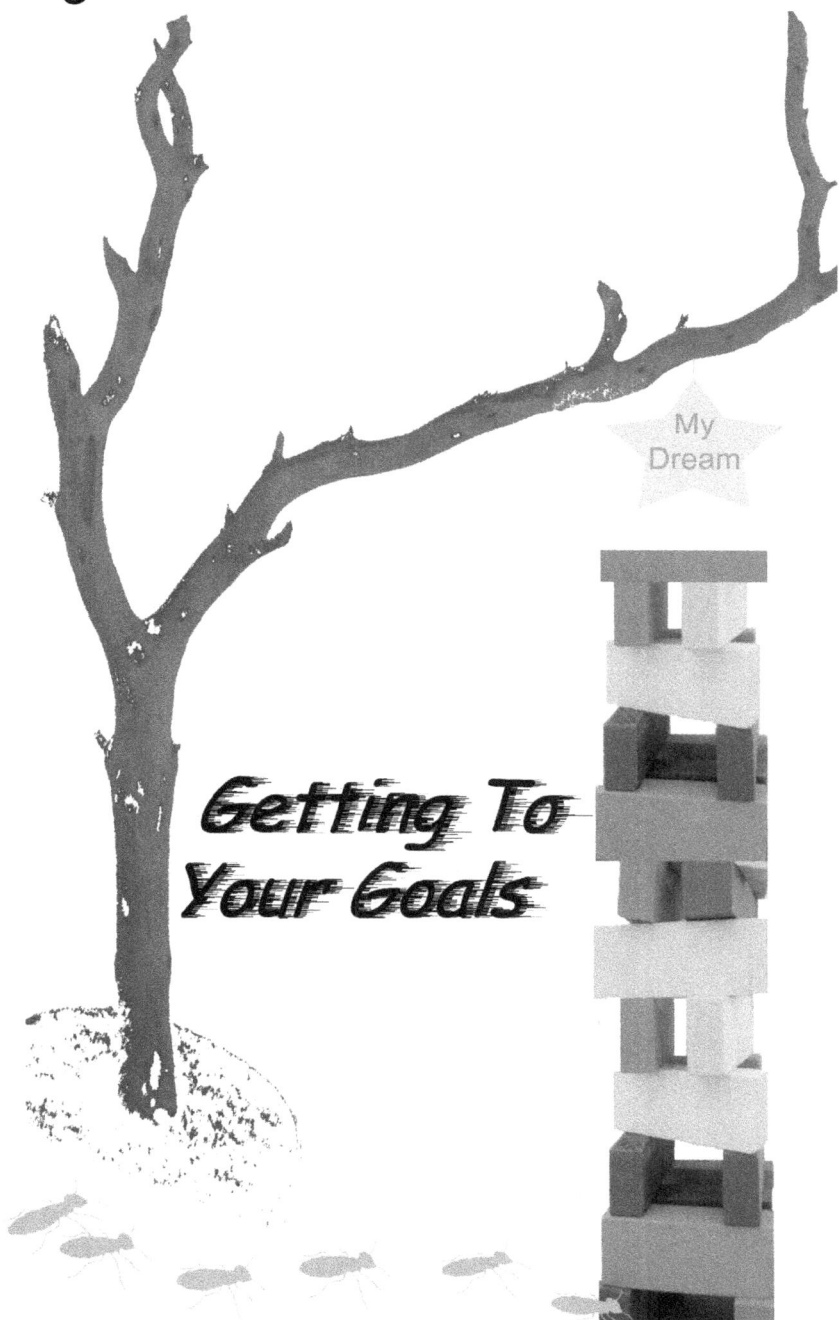

5

My
Dream

Getting To Your Goals

STAND BACK

I don't care what you say, nothin's gonna stop me.
Never give in, I'm on my way, nothin's gonna stop.

Nothin's gonna stop. Never gonna stop.
Nothin's gonna stop me.
Nothin's gonna stop. Never gonna stop.
Nothin's gonna stop me.

CHORUS:
Stand back comin' through
watch out I know what I want.
Stand back comin' through
watch out I know what I want.
Nothin's gonna get in my way. Stand back !
I don't give a damn what you say. Stand back !
Too many things I've got to do
stand back comin' through.

I won't just fade away. Nothin's gonna stop me.
It's my right to live my way. Nothin's gonna stop.

Nothin's gonna stop. Never gonna stop.
Nothin's gonna stop me.
Nothin's gonna stop. Never gonna stop.
Nothin's gonna stop me.

REPEAT CHORUS

Stand back comin' through
watch out I know what I want.
Stand back comin' through watch out!
(REPEAT THIS SECTION)

Stand back. Stand back.

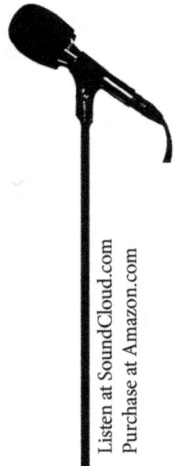

An Explanation of the Opening Graphic

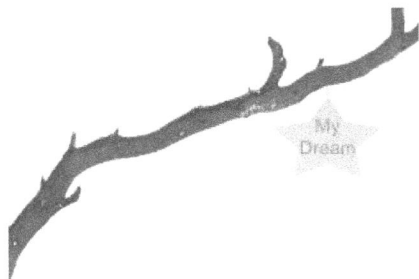

We must often go out on a limb to get to our dreams.

My Dream

These blocks represent the building blocks of the plan that leads you to your dream.

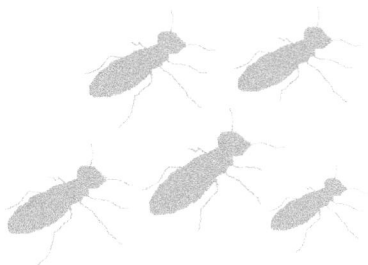

Termites, like doubt and fear, can squeeze through the cracks in your plan and destroy your dreams.

The winds of adversity will test your commitment to your dream and the validity of your plan.

Winds of Adversity

THE BUILDING BLOCKS
OF YOUR PLAN

Action

Risk

Resources

Goals

Passion

What are the key building blocks of your plan? If key elements are missing, your plan will come tumbling down. Add your own ideas, if not listed.

Passion
Goals
Resources
Skills
Talents
Money
Time
Energy
Timing
Risk
Action

THE GLUE
that holds your plan together

DREAMER'S GLUE

INGREDIENTS: Accountability, Adaptability, Ambition, Balance, Belief, Character, Commitment, Confidence, Courage, Desire, Determination, Education, Experience, Faith, Flexibility, Focus, Goals, Hope, Humility, Imagination, Inspiration, Integrity, Measurable progress, Motivation, Passion, Perseverance, Personal Growth, Preparation, Risk Management, Sacrifice, Self knowledge, Self respect, Stress Management, Support System, Values, Vision, Will, Wisdom and Work.

Even if your plan is made from the strongest building blocks it will fall apart if not secured properly. Above are some words that represent the glue that will keep your plan together and your dreams alive. Add other words, if you wish.

TERMITES
THAT CAN DESTROY YOUR DREAM

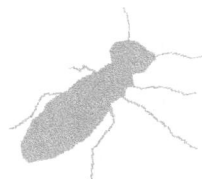

Termites are destructive creatures. They can squeeze through the cracks in your plan and destroy your dream. Below is a list of words that may represent the termites in your life. We all have them. We must identify our termites before we can destroy them. Be vigilant, termites will come back if not kept in check. Add other words to the list, if applicable.

Anxiety
Attitudes
Bad habits
Beliefs
Bitterness
Blame
Boredom
Burnout
Compromised values
Denial
Discontentment
Discouragement
Doubt
Emotion commotion
Excuses
Fault-finding
Fear
Getting off budget
Impatience

Indecision
Jealousy
Juggling too much
Lack of clear vision
Lack of focus
Lack self discipline
Laziness
Life out of balance
Living in the past
Mediocrity
Negativity
No deadlines
No inner peace
Not being yourself
Passivity
Perfectionism

Pessimism
Playing it safe
Pride
Procrastination
Resentment
Resisting Change
Self deception
Self defeat
Self esteem issues
Self pity
Stress
Stubbornness
Tension
Unhealthy lifestyle
Unhealthy risks
Unresolved anger

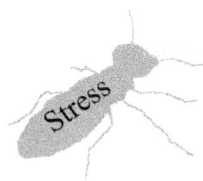

GETTING TO YOUR GOALS

*Decide what you want,
decide what you are willing
to exchange for it.
Establish your priorities
and go to work.*

— H. L. Hunt,
Oil Tycoon

It's fun to fantasize about being this or doing that, but if you wish to turn a dream into reality you must set goals and work through them. The following Goal Worksheet will help you develop a plan to bring your dream to life. Keep in mind that it will take time and probably many revisions to develop a coherent, viable plan for a difficult dream. Be clear in your objectives, but remain flexible in your approach. Not all dreams require extensive planning. Use the Worksheet to get you going but don't let it bog you down. Complete the sections you deem necessary. Start with broad strokes and add more detail as needed.

1. **Define Your Dream:**
   o Clearly define your dream as a specific, measurable goal.

2. **Expectations and Concerns:**
   o Expectations: What do you expect to gain if you are successful?
   o Concerns: What aspects concern you?
   o Thrills: What aspects of pursuing this dream excite you?
   o Impact: What impact will pursuing this dream have on your career, family, finances, health, lifestyle, relationships, time for other things, self esteem, etc.
   o Failure: What might you lose if you fail to reach your

goal? What might you lose if you don't try?

3. **Know Yourself:**
   - o Values: Can you achieve your dream while remaining true to yourself and your values? (See Chapter 2: "How Do You Define Success")
   - o Motivation: What is the driving force or motivation behind your dream? (See Chapter 2: "Understand Your Motivation")
   - o Strengths: With regard to this dream what are your strengths?
   - o Weaknesses: What are your weaknesses?

4. **Gather Information:**
   - o Educate yourself: Where can you gather information about your goals? Include periodicals, workshops, organizations, entrepreneurs, teachers, etc.
   - o Trial Run: Is there a way to "test drive" your dream before taking the plunge?
   - o Needs: List any skills, education, experience and resources you will need.
   - o Money: List ways to raise money for your dream, if needed.

5. **Time and Timing:**
   - o Timing: Are you able, at this time, to give this dream what is required to be successful?
   - o Schedule time: What specific time slots will you commit to pursuing your goals?

6. **Risk:**
   - o Improve your odds: Describe the risks associated with this dream and ways to better your odds for success.

7. **Support:**
   - o Peers: List organizations for people with similar goals.
   - o Mentors: Describe the challenges associated with this

dream and the names of possible mentors who may assist with these challenges.

- o Connections: List any contacts or connections that are critical to your success and how you will make them.
- o Cheerleaders: List people you can count on for encouragement.

8. Roadblocks to Success
- o Rejection: Is there an element of rejection or criticism associated with pursuing your dream? If so, describe it and how you will deal with it.
- o Competition: If you are competing with others for the same dream, what gives you the edge?
- o Temptation: List any temptations that may interfere with reaching your goal, followed by how you will resist them.
- o Sacrifice: Describe any sacrifices that your dream requires.

9. Define Your Action Steps:
- o Describe and prioritize the steps you will take to reach your goal. Start with broad strokes then divide complex steps into a series of simpler ones.
- o Set a specific date of completion for each action step and your overall goal.

10. Measure and Reward Your Progress:
- o Measure your progress: Describe how and when you will measure your progress toward your goal.
- o Reward yourself: List the rewards you will use to keep yourself motivated.

To accomplish great things, we must not only act,
but also dream; not only plan, but also believe.

— Anatole France,
Awarded Nobel Prize for Literature

Reality Check!

It's time to check the validity of your plan. Ask a friend and a mentor to review the plan for validity, feasibility and practicality. A mentor knows the journey; a friend knows you. It may be hard to hear what they have to say, but if you are truly serious about succeeding at your dream, their input could be priceless. If you have holes in your plan, it's better to find out now than to set sail on a sinking ship.

You have teenagers thinking they're going to make millions as NBA stars when that's not realistic for even 1 percent of them. Becoming a scientist or engineer is.

— Dean Kamen,
Inventor of the Segway PT

Develop a Plan "B"

The most successful people are those who are good at Plan B.

— James Yorke,
Mathematician

Remember, you have chosen to pursue a difficult dream. Develop a variation on your dream that is less difficult to achieve yet still fulfilling. If you go into any restaurant in Los Angeles you'll find aspiring actors waiting tables. The harsh reality is: only a very small percentage of actors will make an adequate living from the entertainment industry. The same goes for musicians, writers, athletes, entrepreneurs, inventors, artists, songwriters and the list goes on. What's your Plan "B."

*My dreams are worthless, my plans are dust,
my goals are impossible. All are of no value
unless they are followed by action.*

— Og Mandino,
(He overcame alcoholism
to become a best-selling author.)

- According to collegegrad.com, "Of the nearly 100,000 Screen Actors Guild (SAG) members, only about 50 might be considered stars. The average income that SAG members earn from acting is less than $5,000 a year.... Therefore, most actors must supplement their incomes by holding jobs in other occupations."[1] According to the New York Times, "Only 5 percent of SAG's membership earns more than $75000 a year."[2] Competition for acting jobs is so intense that "only performers with the most stamina and talent will find regular employment."[3]

- A survey by the Physicians' Foundation in 2008 revealed that 49 percent of the 12,000 physicians surveyed said "they'd consider leaving medicine... because there's too much red tape generated from insurance companies and government agencies."[4]

- According to Bureau of Labor Statistics, "most professional athletes' careers last only a few years due to debilitating injuries and age."[5]

- According to the Nashville Songwriters Association Int'l (NSAI), songwriters receive 9.1 cents for a song that sells on an artist's CD. However, this amount is usually split with the publisher, leaving the songwriter only 4.55 cents per CD sold. If the song is co-written with another songwriter each writer receives only 2.275 cents per CD. Therefore, if a songwriter co-writes a cut on a million-selling album, the songwriter earns approximately $22,750.[6]

- According to the Official Website of Minor League Baseball the first contract season salary for players is $1,100/month maximum. After that, it is open to negotiation. Players also receive a $20/day meal allowance.[7]

- According to WikiAnswers.com, the percentage of college athletes who go on to play professionally is 1/5 of 1 percent.[8]

- Mike Gray, Senior Director of Product Design for Hasbro Games cautions game inventors. He says, "Unfortunately, good games don't always sell…. They might have terrible packaging, a bad theme, an awful TV commercial, there might be similar games that are just better, it might come out too late for the buying seasons, or it might be too expensive… all things beyond the inventor's control."[9]

- Television producer and writer, Stephen J. Cannell, offers this sobering fact, "In show business, failure is the principle commerce. For every thousand pitches, ten are bought, and most of those fail."[10]

*I think my first and foremost advice is to have
a very realistic understanding of what making movies is;
how much work it is, how unglamorous it is,
how much tenacity you have to have.*

*— Alex Winter,
actor, director, writer*

IS YOUR PLAN BALANCED, WEAK OR WOBBLY?

We can be so wrapped up in the excitement of pursuing a dream that we don't see the flaws in our plan. Here are some examples of plans that are unbalanced, weak or wobbly:

- You have plenty of passion… but no plan.
- You have passion + a plan… but your plan is faulty.
- You have passion + a plan…
  but insufficient skills or resources.
- You have passion + a plan + skills + resources…
  but you take no action.
- You have passion + a plan + skills + resources + action…
  but your values are compromised.
- You have passion + a plan + skills + action +
  values respected… but your timing is poor.
- You are willing to take a risk, but the risk is unhealthy.
- You have overestimated your talent or skill.
- You have underestimated the difficulty of your dream.
- You are unwilling to make sacrifices for your dream.

Dream About the Stars

What I knew deep in my soul was: the only thing I wanted to work on in my life was space. I would do it any way I could. If I could just translate astronomical tables, I would be happy doing that. If I could sweep the floor around the rocket I would be happy doing that. So it made no difference to me. That was my sustenance. That is my sustenance. And now I run NASA. It doesn't get any better than this.[11]

— Daniel Goldin,
Administrator of NASA

FAITH TO EXPLORE
NEW FRONTIERS

Baruch Blumberg grew up in Brooklyn with a dream of discovering new frontiers like his heroes of the past. The frontiers he chose to explore were those involving medical research. With determination and faith Blumberg's research led him to the discovery of the hepatitis B vaccine which has saved millions of lives. Blumberg said, "when you do basic scientific research, you develop a kind of conviction — a sort of faith — that it's going to have some important application, even when it doesn't appear that way at the initiation of the project."[12]

*If you will call your troubles experiences,
and remember that every experience
develops some latent force within you,
you will grow vigorous and happy,
however adverse your
circumstances may seem to be.*

— John Heywood,
Playwright and Poet

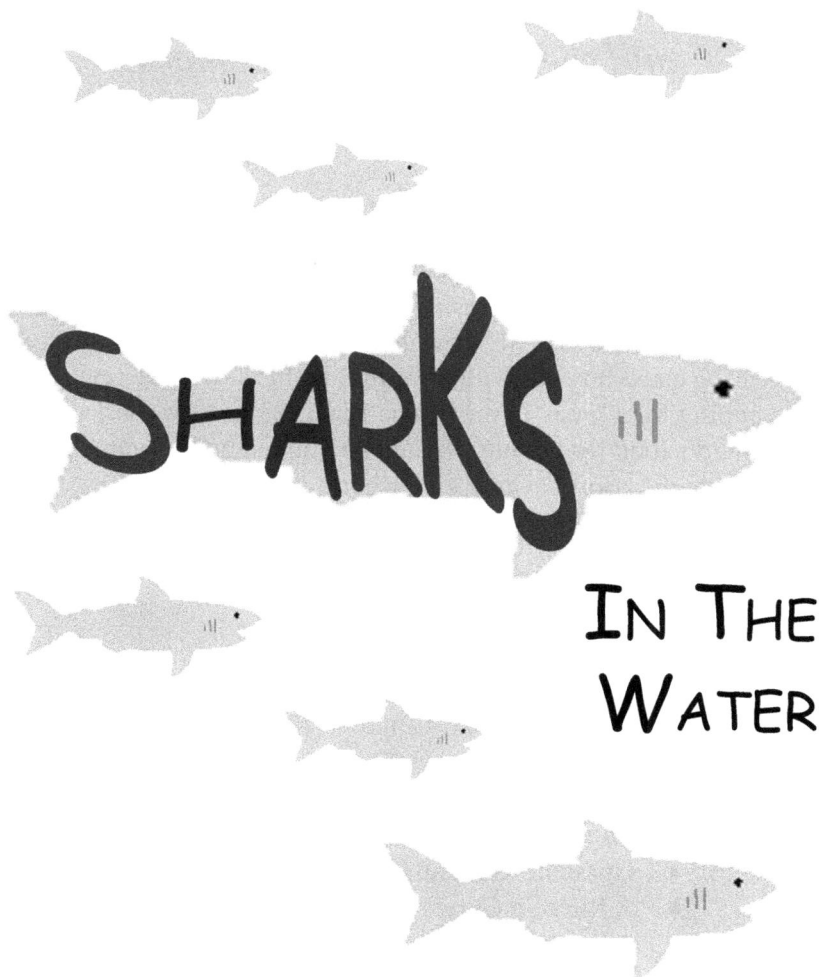

SHARKS

IN THE
WATER

There's a sucker born
every minute.

— P. T. Barnum

There are sharks in the water
and they prey upon dreamers

THE WARNING SIGNS OF A SCAM

Any industry that people dream of being a part of will have its share of sharks. In Nashville, these con artists often sit in restaurants near Music Row looking for a guy sitting alone wearing a cowboy hat with his guitar by his side. The newcomer is hoping for a break in the Music Business and the sharks know it. Sharks look for people who are so blinded by the stars in their eyes that they don't even notice when a con artist is robbing them blind. Watch for these red flags.

- Sounds too good to be true
- A request for secrecy
- A stranger who acts like a friend
- Limited Offer... Limited Time Only
- Advance Payment Required
- Easy Money... Risk Free
- Pressure to act now!
- Guaranteed Results
- A Miracle Cure
- A Promise of financial freedom
- No documentation to substantiate a claim
- A "Tax Free" Investment
- High Pressure
- Won't take "No" for an answer
- Asks leading questions that can only be answered one way... to their benefit
- You are asked to pay a fee for something that should be free[1]

COMMON CONS
AIMED AT PEOPLE WITH A DREAM

Con artists are like cockroaches. They look for cracks in the law where they can hide. This is where they thrive and prey upon our ignorance, kindness, greed and vanity. Con artists commonly try to rip you off for enough money to make it worthwhile for them, but not too much money that you will spend good money after bad pursuing justice. Below are some common cons that are designed to take advantage of people with a dream. Beware!

OFFERING A PROMISE OF FINANCIAL FREEDOM
Many people dream of early retirement and financial security. Beware of people or companies seeking investors declaring that a particular investment is risk free or that they can guarantee a large return on your investment. There are no guarantees when it comes to investing. If someone claims that an investment is tax free verify this with legal and accounting professionals. Review any investment opportunity under the guidance of people who are qualified to assess the risk, and the potential return on your investment.

HEALTH-RELATED CONS
A person with health problems, who dreams of feeling better, might fall victim to a con artist. Another person who dreams of being thinner or having 6-pack abs might be duped by a weight loss product scam. Always consult a health care professional before purchasing products from companies making miraculous claims. You aren't just risking your money; some products may be harmful.

WORK-AT-HOME SCAMS
Common work-at-home scams target people who dream of being their own boss and earning money from home. Some of these scams require you to submit a sample of your work (i.e. needlepoint) to see if you are qualified. They may claim that since they get so many applicants who want to work for them a non-refundable evaluation fee is necessary. This is supposedly done to weed out any applicants

who aren't serious. Often the fee is kept and nobody is ever qualified.

Other scams require you to buy a start-up kit, an employee manual or make some other investment to enable you to work for them. If you are working for them, aren't they supposed to be paying you?

To verify the legitimacy of any questionable company, contact your Attorney General and the Better Business Bureau. Even legitimate home-based businesses must be approached with caution. Often people jump in while they're excited, spending their life savings only to discover they are not cut out for the business.

INVENTION EVALUATION COMPANIES

Who hasn't dreamed of inventing the next million dollar gadget? Invention evaluation companies encourage you to submit your idea for an assessment of its marketability and patentability. It is critical that you look into the qualifications of the company. In 2007, one company was fined $61 million for misleading clients.[2] If you have a unique invention, seek the advice of a reputable patent attorney.

MODELS WANTED

This ad may appeal to our vanity or desire for wealth and fame. Who wouldn't want to be a model? Ads often say they need "real people" types such as children, grandmothers, college students and construction workers. An unscrupulous company may lure you in, but then inform you that you must pay $500 for photographs or sign a contract for modeling classes before you can go on assignment.

THE "SELF PROCLAIMED" EXPERT

This con artist is common in the Entertainment Industry (music, TV, radio, modeling, etc.). Posing as a producer, director, photographer, talent scout, manager, record or film company executive, he or she preys upon people hoping to be discovered. A person can legally call himself almost anything. It's important to verify that he or she is known and respected within their particular industry. Educate yourself about how the industry you are pursuing works. Learn the role of each player and how their role impacts you. For example, who you pay directly for services and who gets paid a percentage of your profits. Libraries offer many free resources to acquire this knowledge.

CHARITABLE DONATIONS

A person with a dream of helping others may be an easy mark for a bogus charity. Check out any solicitor with the Better Business Bureau Wise Giving Alliance. Even with well known charities, it's a good idea to ask how the money is dispersed and what relation the caller has to the organization. Many times only a small portion of the collection goes to the people in need.

CREATIVITY CONTESTS

Many people dream of being a published author, photographer, songwriter, illustrator or poet; and con artists know it. There are endless contests proclaiming to be the gateway into the publishing world. In some contests everyone wins a prize. You get an official

Miracle 2000
Does it all!

Removes Stains! Unclogs Drains!
Will grow hair on a cue ball!
Will melt away those extra pounds!

"best dang fishin' bait I ever seen!"
— Bubba Jones

Developed by NASSA

Special Price: $12.99
Limited Time Offer! Don't miss out!

Miracle 2000
Box A, Snake Oil, CO 12345

Miracle 2000 will change your life!!

looking certificate that means nothing to legitimate publishers. The company then announces that it is publishing a collection of the contest winners for distribution to industry professionals. Many contestants will buy the book to see their work in print. Do some research to ensure that the contest is respected within the industry.

TRAVEL PACKAGE CON
This con is directed toward the person who dreams of seeing the world. Some theives make up travel packages that sound irresistible; but the only person getting out of town is the crook with your money. If you are offered a package deal including airfare, hotel and car rental, contact the other parties involved to verify their participation. Con artists will include the names of legitimate companies in their ads to bolster their scam. Check out any unfamiliar travel agency with the Better Business Bureau and your local Chamber of Commerce.

OVERSEAS JOBS SCAM
An ad for overseas jobs may appeal to a person who dreams of living in an exotic location. Often times the information you order is useless or outdated. A 900 number in the ad may lead to a long recording that keeps you on the phone for a long time. If you call this number be aware that the phone company will bill your account by the minute. 900 numbers can charge up to $50 per call.[3] Know the cost before making the call.

Rev Up Your Passion

I persevered against all odds and against the rules because I believed in my dreams. It would have been more difficult for me to live with that unfulfilled passion than it was to fight to make it happen. Because I held true to my dreams, today I know the feeling of a 5,000 horsepower engine, the feeling of driving over 300 miles-per-hour, and most importantly I know the feeling of being a champion.[4]

Shirley
Muldowney
World Champion Drag Racer

Helpful Resources

Report con artists to the appropriate agencies.
Here are some helpful resources.

Better Business Bureau Headquarters (BBB)
4200 Wilson Blvd., Suite 800, Arlington, VA 22203
Phone: 703-276-0100 Website: www.bbb.org
Description: The BBB has local offices throughout the country. It provides consumer education materials, investigates complaints against companies and works to promote an ethical marketplace by encouraging honest advertising and selling practices.

Better Business Bureau Wise Giving Alliance
(Div. of BBB)
Phone: 703-276-0100
Website: www.bbb.org/us/Wise-Giving/
Description: The BBB Wise Giving Alliance helps donors make informed giving decisions and advances high standards of conduct among organizations that solicit contributions from the public.

Better Business Bureau (Nearest You)
Consult your local listings and write below.

_____
_____
Phone: _____
Website: _____

Federal Trade Commission (FTC)
600 Pennsylvania Avenue, NW, Washington, DC 20580
Phone: 202-326-2222 Website: www.ftc.gov
Description: The Consumer Response Center of the FTC handles consumer protection issues including: Consumer Fraud, Consumer Privacy, Credit Reports, Debt Collection, False or Misleading

Advertising, Internet/Electronic Commerce, Investment Fraud, Leasing, Lending, Mail Order, Telemarketing, Tobacco Advertising and Warranties.

National Association of Attorneys General
2030 M Street NW, 8th Floor, Washington, DC 20036
Phone: 202-326-6000 Website: www.naag.org
Description: State Attorneys General have primary responsibility for the enforcement of their state's consumer protection laws. Every state has a consumer protection statute prohibiting deceptive acts and practices.

> **Attorney General** (For Your State)
> Consult your local listings and write below.
>
> _____
> _____
> Phone: _____
> Website: _____

National Fraud Information Center
Division of National Consumers League
1701 K Street, NW, Suite 1200, Washington, DC 20006
Phone: 202-835-3323 Website: www.fraud.org
Description: Assists consumers in recognizing the signs of telemarketing and internet fraud and in filing complaints.

Awareness
is the key
to protecting yourself
and your dreams.

PUTTING UP WITH PUT DOWNS

LDH

*Keep away from people
who try to belittle your ambitions.
Small people always do that,
but the really great make you feel
that you, too, can become great.*

— Mark Twain

TOMORROW'S HEROES

There are people in this world
who will pull ya down.
They'll tie a rope around your ankles
if your feet ever leave the ground.
Like an anchor they will hold you
when a dream says, "Time to go."
So before your passions drift away
there's somethin' you should know.

CHORUS:
Dreams don't live by other people's rules.
Tomorrow's heroes were yesterday's fools.
Dreams don't live by other people's rules.
The only one they'll listen to is you
yeah, yeah you.

Take a look around you.
All we have was built on dreams.
One man's vision brought the light,
so in darkness we can see.
You may miss the mark many times
before you get it right;
but the only way to truly fail
is to never try.

REPEAT CHORUS (2 times)

You're the only one they'll listen to.

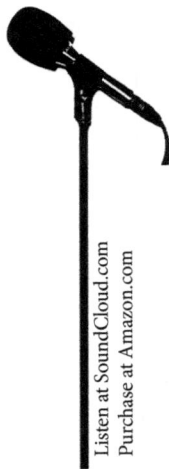

PUTTING UP WITH PUT DOWNS

*First they ignore you, then they laugh at you,
then they fight you, then you win.*

— Mahatma Gandhi,
political and spiritual leader

Putting up with put downs is part of the price you'll pay for stepping away from the crowd to follow a dream. How you respond to a critic will either fuel the fire or squelch it. Former First Lady Eleanor Roosevelt said, "No one can make you feel inferior without your consent." It's true, others may have their opinions, but you don't have to buy in to them. You can't control other people's behavior, but you can control how you react to their actions. Many critics are just looking to get a rise out of you. You can play the role of the puppet and let them pull your strings or you can cut the strings, stand firm and refuse to give away your power. Don't let anyone break your spirit or write you off. Prove them wrong!

CONSIDER THE SOURCE
When you receive criticism, ask yourself if you actually value that particular person's opinion. Maybe he or she is worth listening to, maybe not. You decide. Look for feedback from people whose opinions you respect. It is especially important to find people who have successfully reached the goals you seek. An honest critic, offering constructive criticism, may be your best asset. All you have to do is watch an episode of *American Idol* to see plenty of people who are fooling themselves as to their level of talent. Honest feedback, by critics who care, may be the kick in the pants you need to make real progress toward your dream.

A SHATTERED SPIRIT
Many skeptics are people who have given up on their own dreams.

Therefore, why would you expect them to be supportive? It's sad, but some people are hurting so badly inside that they will try to shatter your spirit so that it matches their own. Forgive them, accept them, but move on! Show, through your actions, that dreams are worth pursuing.

WHAT'S YOUR KRYPTONITE?
People who are able to push our buttons can teach us a lot about ourselves. They show us where we are vulnerable. What's your kryptonite, your weak spot? If what your critics say is hurtful, ask yourself if there is validity to what they are saying. Your critics may have a point. If so, work on your weaknesses and press on.

YOUR COMFORT LEVEL…
MAKES SOME PEOPLE UNCOMFORTABLE
A person who feels the need to put you down may be doing so because he or she feels threatened by you. The mere fact that you are pursuing your dream can make people, who aren't pursuing theirs, uncomfortable. It may be best to keep some of your goals to yourself rather than share them with people who are likely to be critical. Don't let the insecurities of others keep you from your dreams.

SAIL AGAINST THE WIND
Throughout history pioneers have gone against the grain, stepping out of the norm to achieve great things. Robert Fulton was one of these men. He invented the first commercially successful steamship. Napoleon Bonaparte criticized Fulton's dream saying, "You expect a ship to sail against the winds and currents by building a bonfire under her decks? Forgive me, Sir; I have no time for such nonsense."[1] If you step away from the crowd you can expect to be criticized. But don't let it get you down. Create a clear vision of what you want. Set your mind, make a plan and take action.

I'm sure Erik Weihenmayer had a difficult time convincing others that his dream was possible. On May 25, 2001 he became the first blind person to scale Mt. Everest. On August 20, 2008, when Eric stood atop Carstenz Pyramid, the tallest peak in Austral-Asia, Weihenmayer fulfilled his dream to climb the seven highest mountains on each of the seven continents.[2]

MY GRUDGE WON'T BUDGE

Grudges are hurts we write on our hearts. When someone belittles your dreams it's easy to feel justified in holding a grudge. You may be justified, but who are you hurting? Remember, if your grudge won't budge neither will you. Carrying a grudge will wear you out. Learn the power of forgiveness. Forgiveness doesn't excuse their behavior, but it does free you up to move on. Don't let the sludge of a grudge bog you down wasting precious time and energy that you could use toward your dream.

DARK CLOUDS

I know a few people who are only happy when they're miserable. I call them "Dark Clouds." They will cast a shadow over everything and everyone they encounter. These people are able to put a negative spin on anything and will stop at nothing to draw you into the darkness and away from your dreams. When you see "Dark Clouds" coming, take cover!

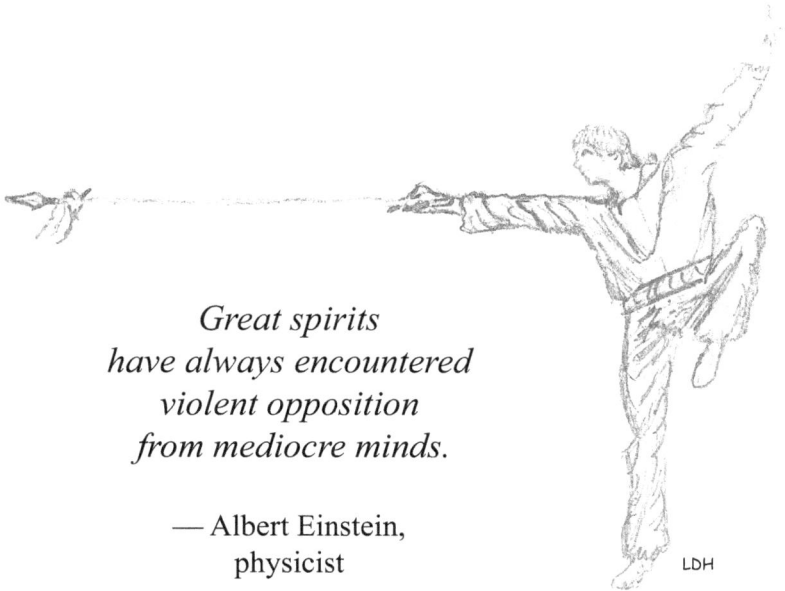

*Great spirits
have always encountered
violent opposition
from mediocre minds.*

— Albert Einstein,
physicist

LDH

SAYS WHO?

Below are some scathing comments by critics. The people on the receiving end of these criticisms could have curled up into a ball and given up; but they didn't. Neither should you. Don't cave in to criticism.

❖ Thomas Edison discounted the value of radio insisting that "the radio craze… will die out in time."[3]

❖ The London Critic criticized Walt Whitman saying he "is as unacquainted with art as a hog is with mathematics."[4]

❖ Sylvia Earle accomplished her dream of becoming an Undersea Explorer but acknowledged that throughout her life she has felt pressure to conform to what society considers acceptable behavior. She said, "At various points along the way, the fact that I am a woman was held up to me as a reason why I couldn't do this or that or the other thing." Earle went on to lead more than 60 expeditions, logged more than 6000 hours underwater and set a record for solo diving to a depth of 1000 meters.[5]

❖ The New York Times ran a review of the book *Raise the Titanic* by Clive Cussler. It read, "If good books get roses, and bad books get skunks, Cussler's book would receive four skunks."[6] The book became a best seller.

Pioneers
Are Often Persecuted

Be prepared that your new idea will not always be welcome. As a very young assistant at the University of Groningen, when I told the chief assistant that I was going to make an artificial kidney, he became very, very mad. What I should do, he said, was just like every other young assistant: Do what he told us. But my old professor listened, and let me do it.[7]

— Willem Kolff,
Pioneer of Artificial Organs

MOSQUITO BITES

Some critics are like mosquitoes. They buzz around, poking and prodding, looking for blood. The more you swat and complain, the more they attack. The best repellent for this type of pest is to ignore or avoid them. If they sense they're getting to you — if they smell blood — they'll never give up. On the other hand, if you don't even acknowledge them, these pests are likely to give up and look for someone else to bug.

Never be bullied into silence.
Never allow yourself to be made a victim.
Accept no one's definition of your life; define yourself.

— Harvey Fierstein,
actor and playwright

He Who Laughs Last...

- Les Paul was laughed at for experimenting with the electric guitar.[8]

- George Foreman was ridiculed for pursuing the Heavyweight Boxing Championship at the age of 45. In the tenth round he knocked out 26-year-old Michael Moorer who had been previously undefeated.[9]

- Louis Pasteur was laughed at for his theory of germs.[10]

- In 1938, Parker Brothers executives rejected the game of Monopoly citing 52 design flaws. It is now the best selling board-game in the world selling over 200 million copies. An estimated 500 million people have played the game.[11]

I never doubted my ability,
but when you hear all your life you're inferior,
it makes you wonder if the other guys
have something you've never seen before.
If they do, I'm still looking for it.

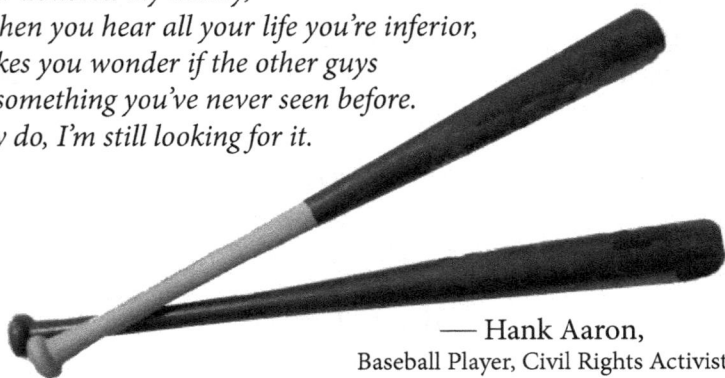

—— Hank Aaron,
Baseball Player, Civil Rights Activist

- 8 -

LDH

WATCH YOUR THOUGHTS

*One day you may catch yourself
smiling at the voice in your head,
as you would smile at the antics of a child.
This means you no longer take
the content of your mind all that seriously,
as your sense of self does not depend on it.*

— Eckhart Tolle,
motivational speaker and writer

NO ROOM FOR NEGATIVES

I'm not gonna let you get me down.
Pickin' my soul up off the ground.
You're not gonna get the best of me . . . No!
Givin' defeat the 3rd degree.

I'll never stop . . . Oh no...
to get caught in the run-around
and I won't let bad attitudes get me down.

CHORUS:
Absolutely positive I've got no room for negatives.
Absolutely positive I've got no room for negatives.

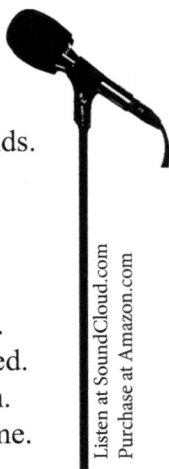

I'm not gonna dress my life in gray.
I'll never douse my spirit's flame.
I know what I want, won't be denied.
Only one goal: peace of mind.

There's no guarantee I'll find serenity
but I won't be my own worst enemy!

REPEAT CHORUS

Here's a little message for you cynical minds.
All I've got to say is . . . bye bye!

REPEAT CHORUS

I'm walkin' where fear and faith collide.
I know what I want and I will not be denied.
I'm focused and driven by a dream, yeah.
I know what I want and I know it's up to me.

REPEAT SECTION ABOVE

Absolutely positive I've got no room for negatives.

THE PEARL

I am feeling great.
I am feeling wonderful.
I am feeling fine. Oh so fine.
My life is truly blessed,
better than I'd ever guessed
and getting better all the time.

CHORUS:
Since I made up my mind,
I can choose the way I view my world.
I can decide to look past the pain
to find the pearl.

I'm learning as I grow,
trusting life, letting go.
Looking at the world
through different eyes.
No matter what life brings,
I have faith for better things,
knowin' soon the sun will shine.

REPEAT CHORUS

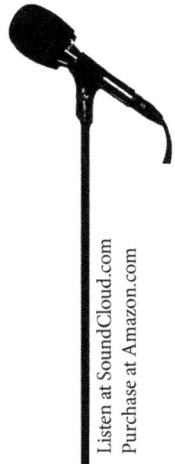

I'm seein' life in a different light now.

REPEAT CHORUS

WATCH YOUR THOUGHTS

Many highly intelligent people are poor thinkers.
Many people of average intelligence are skilled thinkers.
The power of the car is separate from the way the car is driven.

— Edward De Bono,
physician, author, inventor

Don't underestimate the power of your thoughts. Our minds can keep us calm and focused amid turmoil, or turn calm into calamity. Our thoughts shape our world. When we change our perception of our world, our lives and ourselves — we change our world, our lives and ourselves.

Dr. Masaru Emoto discovered that molecules of water are affected by thought. When water molecules are exposed to different thoughts they change shape. He captures this phenomenon with amazing photographic clarity in his NY Times Best selling book, "The Hidden Messages in Water." Since our bodies are 70% water we need to consider the impact that our thoughts are having upon us, our health and our dreams. It is critical that we realize we have the power to change those thoughts that are working against us.[1]

LOOK PAST THE PROBLEMS

Actor Gary Cooper was offered the lead role in *Gone with the Wind* but he chose to look at the problems associated with the role instead of the possibilities. He turned down the part saying, "I'm just glad it'll be Clark Gable who's falling on his face and not Gary Cooper."[2] Well, Clark Gable didn't fall on his face and "Gone with the Wind" reached monumental success. Cooper's attitude cost him greatly.

Lewis E. Waterman worked as an insurance salesman. He had just closed a deal, his client was ready to sign the contract, but his pen leaked ruining the document. By the time Waterman returned with a new contract, the customer had changed his mind. Fed up with losing a sale due to the poor quality of the writing utensils of the time,

Waterman looked past the problem to the possibilities. He resigned from his job and put all his efforts into developing his new invention: the Fountain Pen.[3]

Ole Evinrude was picnicking with his sweetheart Bessie on a small island in Lake Michigan. When Bessie decided she wanted some ice cream Ole rowed to shore. By the time he got back the ice cream had melted. This gave Ole an idea. He built an outboard motor for his rowboat and gave birth to the Evinrude Outboard Motor Company.[4] What problems are you facing that could be turned into opportunities by making a change in perspective?

REFLEXIVE THINKING

Athletes must often learn to override a reflex that interferes with performance. For example, a pitching coach may notice a hitch or anomaly in a pitcher's throwing motion. Knowing that this hitch could lead to injury, the coach instructs the pitcher about how to make a change. Through repetition the athlete can override the tendency to return to the old habit and substitute a new, healthier one.

When it comes to our thinking, most of us have hitches – thinking

When analyzing a problem, look at it from up close,
at a distance and with your peripheral vision.
Stare up at it, down upon it
and then cross-eyed
before you come to any conclusions.

But especially make sure
that your glasses aren't
dirtied with the dust of ego
or tainted
by the fog of prejudice.

LDH

habits that hold us back. If someone suddenly tossed you a ball you'd probably, out of reflex, try to catch it. If the ball was on fire you would jump out of the way to avoid it. Our minds are constantly tossing us thoughts. Not every thought should be caught, held and examined. Some thoughts are not worth catching. Some of us reflexively turn to worry, self pity or negativity while others turn to faith, courage and optimism. Once we recognize that we have a thinking problem we must work to substitute new healthier ways of thinking. Old habits die hard, but with consistent practice we can change our thought reflexes to be healthier and more productive.

REHEARSE SUCCESS

Our expectations color our experience. If you expect to fail at your dream you probably will. Many of us actually lower our expectations so we won't be disappointed if things don't work out the way we would hope. One day, I went golfing with a friend. He did well on the first hole, then, dejectedly said, "Whenever I do well on the first hole, it's all downhill from there." He was right, his game disintegrated. He talked himself into failing. Walk into any new experience with an open mind by checking any negative expectations at the door.

REGRETS, I'VE HAD A FEW

How much of our lives do we spend dwelling on past mistakes or failures thinking, "If only I…" or "I should have…" It's kind of like bringing a horse to a full gallop then turning backwards in the saddle. We can get so focused on where we have been that we don't see the cliff ahead of us.

MAKE UP YOUR MIND

Make a solemn declaration of what you want for your life and then remind yourself daily. Use the following example to help you write your own.

"I accept responsibility for my life, health, happiness and dreams. I use my time, money and energy wisely. I will not waste my life. If I want something, I make a plan to get it and then implement that plan. I accept myself as I am, as I work to become who I choose to be. I no longer blame others or my circumstances. I do the best I can with whatever I have available at the moment, and am satisfied. I love, respect, honor, forgive and accept myself. The only time I have is now so I use my time wisely. I choose to see a world filled with love, peace, opportunity, excitement and success."

SELF TALK

What do you say when you talk to yourself? We are often much harder on ourselves than we would be on someone else. You may need to rethink your thinking. In times of struggle encourage yourself as you would a friend in the same situation. Beating yourself up for mistakes or fears won't get you any closer to your dream.

Tied Up In

"Nots"

When things aren't working with respect to my dream, I sometimes get discouraged. I begin to focus on what I cannot do, rather than what I can do... who I am not, rather than who I am... what I do not have, rather than what I do have. One "not" can turn into many "nots." James V. Kimsey, founder of America Online was criticized by his colleagues when he decided to launch AOL. He heard comments like, "Why are you fooling around with this thing? Why do you think this is ever going to amount to anything?"[5] The success of AOL proves that he did not allow other people's "nots" to tie up his thinking. Look for any limitations in your thinking that are hindering your progress toward your dreams. Start untying your "nots."

No Vacancy

Who's livin' inside your head and messin' with your dream?

A common tactic used in competitive sports is to try to psych out your opponent. If your opponent is able to get inside your head he or she gains a mental advantage. Throughout our lives we will encounter many people who are trying to gain access. Some people we gladly welcome in while others seem to sneak in without our knowledge or permission. Anyone living in your head will influence your thinking and, therefore, have an enormous impact upon your life. Some of your cranial residents may include: a teacher who recognized your talent, an uncle who said you'd never amount to anything, a coach who pushed you to excel, a neighbor who called you a dreamer and so on. It can get crowded up there.

Each person in our head is endowed with a certain level of influence. We give some people more power over us than others. For example, have you ever had an experience when you received positive support from many people about a project you were doing, yet one person responded negatively? Even though you had ten people pulling for you and only one person pulling against you, you gave that one person's opinion super-human strength. You allowed it to drown out all the other feedback. It's important to remember that we control the space between our ears and have the authority to evict destructive tenants. We can then choose to offer that space to more supportive people. So the next time a critic comes knocking at your door, put out the "No Vacancy" sign.

MIND MUSCLES

By repeating specific exercises over and over again bodybuilders can sculpt their muscles in a particular way. The same goes for our thinking. The thoughts we dwell on over and over again, like the exercises of the bodybuilder, shape our mind. By dwelling on a thought we are sculpting our perceptions, attitudes and expectations around that thought. Practice math and you will get better at math. Practice anxiety or anger and you'll get better at finding things to be anxious or angry about. Practice faith and you will find it easier to reject doubt. The more you exercise your mind with healthy thoughts, the easier it becomes to recognize and reject those thoughts that are detrimental to your dreams. A difficult dream requires a strong mind. So remember, just as a bodybuilder must maintain an exercise program to retain his or her physical strength, we also must work to maintain a strong mind. So, if your mind feels a little flabby, start exercising!

Troubles are a lot like babies. . .
they grow larger if you nurse them.

— Anonymous

MOOD ELEVATOR

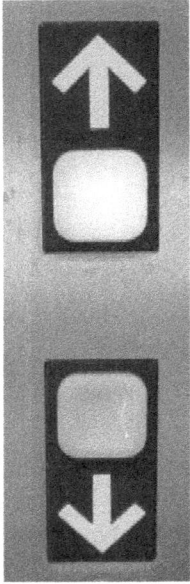

Be prepared for days when you are not in the mood to work on your goals. Sometimes we need a break. Other times we need to lift our spirits and press on. Grab a shoe box and create a Mood Elevator Kit. It will come in handy on those days when you need a little inspiration and motivation. Here are some things to include:

- Index cards with inspirational quotes
- Cards and letters that are special to you
- Inspirational books, articles and poems
- Uplifting pictures, music and movies
- Things that make you laugh or smile

CREATE THESE LISTS:
- A list of the reasons why you want to succeed at your dream
- A list of people you find inspiring
- A list of people you can count on to lift your spirits
- A list of mood elevating activities
- A list of things for which you are thankful
- A list of comforting foods and places
- A list of negative influences to be avoided

I don't wait for moods.
You accomplish nothing if you do that.
Your mind must know
it has to get down to work.

— Pearl Buck,
missionary and writer

- 9 -

DARE TO PERSEVERE

*A rock pile
ceases to be
a rock pile
the moment
a single man
contemplates it,
bearing within him
the image
of a cathedral.*

— Antoine
De Saint-Exupery

HAVE YOU GOT WHAT IT TAKES?

The time will come when you just can't run,
you've gotta fight for what you believe.
Stand your ground firm and proud. Dare to achieve.
It's the only way to be what you wanna be.
You've gotta take the gamble if you want the victory.

CHORUS:
Have you got what it takes to be a champion?
Courage to fight when nothin's going . . .
Got what it takes to be a champion?
Courage to fight when nothin's going right.

A voice within says you must begin to give life to a dream.
If you dare to persevere you can succeed.
It's the only way to be what you wanna be.
You've gotta take the gamble
if you want the victory.

REPEAT CHORUS

Right from the start
somethin' says it's destiny.
You feel it in your heart.
Now's the time to start.
Ask yourself . . .

REPEAT CHORUS

You're a champion... a champion
You're a champion...

It's time to fight!

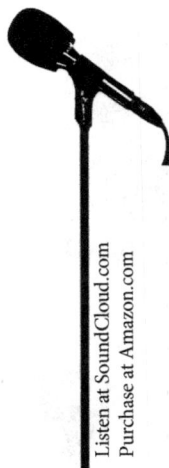

Listen at SoundCloud.com
Purchase at Amazon.com

DARE TO PERSEVERE

*Adversity causes
some men to break,
others to break records.*

— William A. Ward,
author and columnist

Everyone has the potential to succeed at whatever he or she chooses, but potential is not the biggest factor. The drive to develop your potential is the determining factor of success. It takes guts to go after a dream. Here are some examples of people who dared to persevere. You'll discover: the struggle is the spice that brings your dreams to life.

- Laura Hillenbrand suffered from an extreme case of chronic fatigue syndrome. At times, all she could move were her eyelids. She dreamed of being an author and set up an office in her bed. With ingenuity and perseverance she wrote "Seabiscuit."[1]

- In 1927, Eduard Haas invented Pez as a substitute to cigarettes. The idea didn't sell, so he repackaged Pez as a children's toy with cartoon heads and fruit flavored candy. Haas bounced back from defeat, tweaked his idea and created a huge market for his product.[2]

EVERYONE STUMBLES
We will all stumble and fall. It's just a part of life. Learn from and appreciate your failures. Many times we do our best, yet still beat ourselves up as if we could have done better. All this does is waste time and energy that could be used to move forward. The value of success would not be appreciated if you could not fail, and is valued more if you have failed. Everyone stumbles and falls... winners just

keep getting up.

PROFIT FROM YOUR PREDICAMENT
Every problem we encounter contains the seed of opportunity. If you are experiencing a particular problem, others are too. Some people capitalize on our problems by finding solutions they can sell. Most entrepreneurs are simply people who get paid for providing a product or service that solves another person's problem.

With a baby in her arms most of the time, Lillian Moller Gilbreth, a mother of 12, hardly ever had an extra hand free. She profited from her predicament by inventing the trash can with step-on lid opener and the electric food mixer.[3]

PURSUE YOUR PASSION
Sometimes we pursue a dream without knowing the true extent of the challenges we will face or the sacrifices that are required to turn that dream into reality. Will you continue to pursue your passion even if you never reach the level of achievement that society considers successful? For myself, I know that I need to create as much as I need to breathe. So I will always be creating, no matter what. Picasso referred to his passion for painting in this way. "If they took away all my paints, I'd use pastels, if they took away my pastels, I'd use crayons, if they took away my crayons, I'd use a pencil. If they put me in a cell, and stripped me of everything, I'd spit on my finger and draw on the wall."

EXPECT A DIP BEFORE A RISE
Have you ever bought a new gadget because you thought it would make your life easier? Initially, if you struggle with this new tool, you may wonder if you made a mistake in purchasing it. When things get worse before they get better, I call this a "dip before a rise." This phenomenon often occurs when we make changes in our lives. Things often get tougher before they get better. If your plan is sound, hold firm to your decision to change and expect things to turn around. If you go into a change knowing that things are likely to get worse before they get better, you can plan accordingly and are less likely to give up in frustration. Nobody likes change, but it's a necessary part of pursuing a difficult dream.

RECOVER FROM REJECTION

Many people have attempted to scale the mountain of success. Most have been forced to rappel to safety. An incomplete expedition is not a failure. The experience gained from the attempt will support your next attack upon the summit. Recover from your rejections and press on.

- Dr. Seuss's book "And to Think That I Saw It on Mulberry Street" was rejected 27 times before being published. At the time of his death, in 1991, Dr. Seuss had sold over 20 million copies of his books.[4]

- Colonel Sanders, the founder of Kentucky Fried Chicken, was rejected 1,009 times before he found a buyer for his chicken recipe.[5]

- Jimmy Denny, manager of the Grand Ole Opry, fired Elvis Presley after one performance saying, "You ain't goin' nowhere, son. You ought to go back to drivin' a truck."[6]

- Stan Smith set a goal to become a ball boy for a Davis Cup tennis match. He tried out but was rejected because he was considered to be too awkward and clumsy to do the job. Smith overcame this rejection and later in life went on to earn the ranking of the number one tennis player in the world.[7]

- Thomas Edison's first invention, the Electric Vote Counter was rejected by politicians because the slower process of counting votes gave them more time to influence voters. Edison went on to file 1,093 patents.[8]

- After an audition, Decca Records executives rejected The Beatles, saying that "guitar groups are on the way out."[9]

STORMY TIMES

My Dream

Winds of Adversity

Adversity is inevitable. The winds of adversity may knock you down or push you off course. The rains of misfortune may dissolve the glue that holds your plan together. Will your dream weather the storm? It's your choice. Here are some examples of winds of adversity and rains of misfortune:

Bad luck	*Distractions*	*Problems*
Betrayal	*Failure*	*Rejection*
Burdens	*Family matters*	*Resistance*
Challenges	*Glass ceilings*	*Roadblocks*
Change	*Hard times*	*Setbacks*
Closed doors	*Health problems*	*Scarce resources*
Competition	*Injustice*	*Skeptics*
Complications	*Miscalculations*	*Strained relationships*
Con artists	*Misfortune*	*Temptation*
Critics	*Mistakes*	*Trauma*
Dead ends	*Obstacles*	*Troubles*
Delays	*Opposition*	*Unfairness*
Detours	*Pressure*	
Disappointment	*Peer pressure*	

THE BENEFITS OF ADVERSITY

- Adversity challenges your commitment to your dream, yourself and your values.
- Adversity bends you in new ways developing your flexibility and ingenuity for future challenges.
- Adversity wakes you up to where you are weak and heightens your awareness of things that threaten your success.
- Adversity forces you to expand your thinking, question your assumptions, and look for answers in places that you normally wouldn't look.
- Adversity asks you to decide what you are willing to sacrifice to get to your goals.
- Adversity tests your will, resilience, character, self discipline, patience and faith.
- Adversity reveals your true motivation.
- Adversity tests the validity, feasibility and practicality of your plan.
- Adversity pushes you to set priorities and sharpen your focus.
- Adversity challenges you to grow and to grow up.
- The threat of adversity pushes you to be proactive instead of merely reactive.

WHAT OTHERS SAY
ABOUT ADVERSITY

- Walt Disney, animation pioneer: *"You may not realize it when it happens, but a kick in the teeth may be the best thing in the world for you."*

- Leonardo da Vinci, Renaissance man: *"Obstacles cannot crush me. Every obstacle yields to stern resolve. He who is fixed to a star does not change his mind."*

- Oprah Winfrey, media personality: *"Turn your wounds into wisdom."*

- Duke Ellington, musician: *"A problem is a chance for you to do your best."*

- Jonas Salk, medical researcher: *"I have had dreams and I have had nightmares, but I have conquered my nightmares because of my dreams."*

- J. C. Penney, entrepreneur: *"I would never have amounted to anything were it not for adversity. I was forced to come up the hard way."*

- Lance Armstrong, cyclist: *"Cancer taught me to plan for more purposeful living, and that in turn taught me how to train and how to win more purposefully."*

- John F. Kennedy, U.S. President: *"When written in Chinese the word "crisis" is composed of two characters — one represents danger and the other represents opportunity."*

- Confucius, philosopher: *"When it is obvious that the goals cannot be reached, don't adjust the goals, adjust the action steps."*

- Helen Keller, (born deaf and blind) author, political activist and lecturer: *"Character cannot be developed in ease and quiet. Only through experience of trial and suffering can the soul be strengthened, ambition inspired and success achieved."*

Slow Start... Big Finish

- Gillette sold only 51 disposable razor sets the first year on the market.[10]

- Tiffany & Co. Jewelers' first day sales totaled $4.98.[11]

- Abraham Lincoln suffered eight defeats for election to public office, two business failures and a nervous breakdown before being elected President of the United States.[12]

- Coca Cola sales averaged 9 drinks per day in its first year.[13]

- Attorney Maxcy Filer passed the bar exam on his 48th attempt. It took over 25 years.[14]

- Noah Webster began working on the Webster's Dictionary at age 43; he finished 27 years later at age 70.[15]

- Comedian Robin Williams was voted "Least Likely to Succeed" by his high school classmates.[16]

- Oprah Winfrey was told she was not fit for television.[17]

- Walter Cronkite was told it would be best that he forget about being a broadcaster.[18]

- Mary Kay Ash's first home show of skin care products resulted in $1.50 in sales.[19]

- Warren Buffet's application to the Harvard Business School was rejected.[20]

- Sandra Day O'Connor graduated at the top of her class from Stanford Law School, but no law firm in California would hire her because of her gender.[21]

- Three out of the first five Woolworth's Stores failed.[22]

FEAR

Dont let the voice of fear drown out the call of your heart.

– LDH

No Regrets

My philosophy has always been: I never want to look back and say something didn't work because I didn't try hard enough. There are enough things working against you – bad luck and things – that you have no control over. The one thing you can control is how hard you work.[6]

– Scott Adams,
creator of the cartoon "Dilbert"

10

FEELS LIKE YOU'RE GETTING NOWHERE

*Flaming enthusiasm,
backed up by
horse sense
and persistence,
is the quality
that most frequently
makes for success.*

— Dale Carnegie,
author
and lecturer

LDH

DON'T WRESTLE WITH THE ROAD

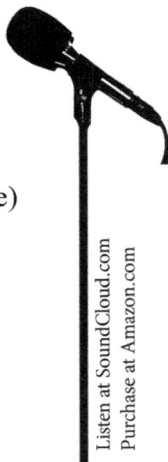

Runnin' around with your head in your hands.
Forced to juggle life's demands.
Got no time to wonder why
the price of life is getting so high.
And you never seem to find peace of mind... No!
Feels like you must have been betrayed.
When you're feelin' this way...

CHORUS:
Take it smooth, slow and easy
don't wrestle with the road. Let go.
Take a break from your journey
and rest your weary soul.
Don't wrestle with the road. (Repeat Line)

Drivin' blind on a road with no end.
Seldom knowing where it bends.
Got no sense of where you are,
where you're going, or how far.
So many miles spent on the road
they're taking they're toll.
There's just one thing left to do.
Take a time-out for you. And...

REPEAT CHORUS

Yes, there will be detours. Most you will not see.
They'll mess with your emotions
and knock you off your feet.
Signs say, "Don't stop." Signs say, "Don't go."
What'cha gonna do, when the signs within you say,
"Take some time for you?"

REPEAT CHORUS

Don't wrestle with the road.

FEELS LIKE YOU'RE GETTING NOWHERE

When we feel stuck, going nowhere,
even starting to slip backward;
we may actually be backing up
to get a running start.

— Dan Millman,
trampoline champion and author

What is your system for measuring progress? If you don't have a system, how do you know if you are getting ahead or not? Movement doesn't necessarily mean progress. You could be going in circles. Select goals that are clearly measurable. Determine how and when you will measure your progress and when you expect to complete each goal. Break long-term goals into a series of short-term goals. For example: a college degree is completed one semester or one course at a time.

THE NEXT HURDLE

We can get so focused on the finish line that when it appears out of reach, we feel stagnant. It's important to clearly define your current, attainable short-term challenge and then decide what steps you will take to work through it. Once there, define your next short-term goal and so on. By thinking about the next hurdle rather than the multitude of hurdles still ahead, you can keep things manageable and in the proper perspective.

EXAMINE THE EVIDENCE

Crime Scene Investigators must present evidence to make their case in court. Feelings don't count. Are you truly getting nowhere or does it just feel that way? What evidence do you have to assess your progress toward your dream? Look at the evidence. If the evidence reveals that you are truly getting nowhere then you need to make changes. Many times you are making progress; it just doesn't feel that way. You may be inching along but not realize it because you fail to acknowledge your small successes. Give yourself credit for any progress you make no matter how small.

MOMENTUM

Progress toward a difficult dream can be slow at times. During these times it's helpful to work on projects that are easier to accomplish so that you get a sense of completion. Use the momentum from that success to carry you into the next project and so on. It's very important to feel like you are always moving forward.

BLIND OPTIMISM

When we first decide to pursue a dream we begin on an emotional high. This blind optimism makes us feel like we can conquer the world. When the excitement wears off we may discover that pursuing our dream is much more difficult than first imagined. If this is true for you, it's time to renew your commitment to this dream or let it go. If you choose to stick with it you will need to review and revise your goal worksheet and action plan.

GROWTH IS REQUIRED

When you feel you are not progressing toward your dream, it may indicate the need for personal growth. You may need to further your education, change a self defeating habit or question an assumption. Doing the work necessary to remove any roadblock-to-success is of critical importance. Give yourself credit for doing this difficult work and recognize it as progress.

CHECK YOUR COMMITMENT LEVEL

When you feel like you are getting nowhere it is useful to ask yourself if you are still as committed to your dream as you were when you started? Are you committed enough to be successful? Review your statement of commitment in Chapter 1. Are there any commitments that you have failed to honor?

TRUSTING A FAULTY MAP

If you feel like you're getting nowhere, you may be right. Your action plan, the roadmap that leads you to your dream, may be flawed. If your plan is weak or wrong, you'll end up lost or wandering around in circles. Key elements could be missing from your plan and therefore inhibiting your progress. It would be helpful, at this time, to seek input from a mentor. He or she can look at your plan and help you revise it, if necessary. Remember, it's okay to ask for directions.

AVOIDING UNCOMFORTABLE STEPS

Take a look at the individual action steps within your plan. You may be stagnant because you are avoiding uncomfortable steps, tasks or decisions. For example, as a songwriter I can write a drawer full of songs; but, if my goal is for others to hear my music, I have to take a risk and put it out there. There is no way around it. Fear can cause us to avoid certain steps that are required to reach our goal.

POOR FLEXIBILITY

Sometimes our goals are so rigidly defined that we overlook opportunities and pathways to our dream that would move us forward. We can make things harder on ourselves by setting goals that are unrealistic, setting standards that are unachievable, and by placing too many demands on ourselves or others. When you feel stuck, re-assess your goals. Make them more practical, flexible and manageable. If you are biting off more than you can chew, try taking smaller bites. Plans can be changed, deadlines can be extended. Make adjustments, set a healthy pace and keep moving forward. You may be stuck because you are stuck in your ways. Be flexible.

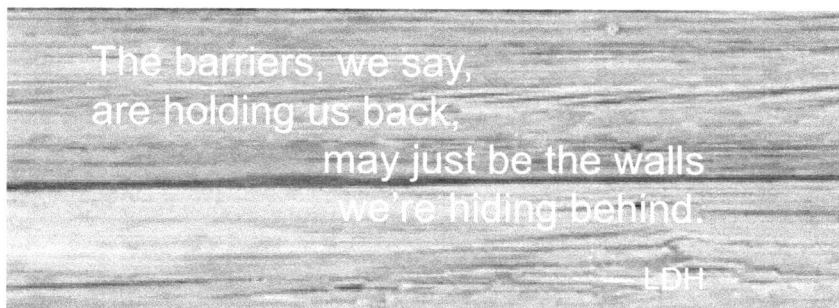

> The barriers, we say,
> are holding us back,
> may just be the walls
> we're hiding behind.
>
> —LDH

FIND PLEASURE IN THE PURSUIT

When success doesn't come quickly, or as expected, it's easy to feel like you are failing or getting nowhere. Remember, you have chosen to pursue a difficult dream. You are already more successful than most people because most people will never even try. Give yourself credit, find contentment in where you are, and learn to enjoy the journey. We often waste an enormous amount of time and energy feeling discontented because we are not where we want to be. Contentment doesn't mean settling for less, but it does mean finding peace and satisfaction in where you are, while you advance to where you would like to be.

A FAULTY SUPPORT SYSTEM

Is your support system comprised of too many "yes men" who are feeding your ego? Are you avoiding talking to a proper mentor because you are afraid he or she may say something that you don't want to hear? If you feel like you're getting nowhere it may be time to consult an expert.

STOP BITCHIN' AND MOANIN' . . .
START SWITCHIN' AND GROWIN'

If you have enough time and energy to complain, you have enough time and energy to change. Even if you can't immediately change your circumstances you can always change your attitude. If you are not happy with where you are at the moment, view your present circumstances as a necessary stepping stone to get where you want to go. Learn as much as you can from the present and keep pressing toward your goal.

FEELING POWERLESS?

If you're feeling powerless, maybe you are. Ask yourself, "What aspects of my dream are within my control and what aspects are not?" Make a list of each. Work on those things that are within your control. You may be getting

nowhere because you are trying to control something that you have no control over.

HOPE ON A ROPE

Is your thinking lifting you up or pulling you down? When we are going through a difficult period it's easy to become overly focused on what is not working with respect to our dream, while ignoring what is working. Our mindset plays a huge role in whether we stay hopeful or feel hopeless. Hopelessness does not secure its grip when we try something and fail. Only when we decide that it can't be done does hopelessness choke out hope. So carry hope on a rope and use it to pull yourself up when you get that sinking feeling.

OUT OF BALANCE

Has your life shifted out of balance? If it has, this could be inhibiting your progress toward your goals. Take a broad look at your life. Are there areas that you have put on hold that are now crying out for attention? If so, you'll need to work to bring your life into a better balance. Once you do, you'll find yourself moving forward again. For more ideas refer to the chapter entitled, "A Healthy Balance."

PULLING WEEDS

During a severe drought in Florida, authorities imposed extreme water restrictions. This took its toll on my lawn but the weeds seemed to thrive. Even when the rain finally came, the weeds had established themselves so well that my grass struggled to recover. During periods when you feel like you're getting nowhere, it may be helpful to look for any weeds in your life that are stunting your growth and preventing you from moving forward. Weeds come in many forms including: attitudes, beliefs, behaviors, habits, people, activities and so on. It is critical to remove any weeds that are choking the life out of your dream.

SETTING STANDARDS

Sometimes we seek the perfect solution to a problem when an adequate solution is sufficient enough to keep us moving forward. Other times, we get mired in mediocrity by accepting low standards and our dream pays the price. Are your standards set too high or not high enough? Either extreme can inhibit your progress toward your dream.

THE THRILL IS GONE

Have you stopped believing you can do it? When we are excited about a new dream, it's easy to stay motivated. But when times get tough, our true motivation, or lack of it, will be revealed. Take another look at the motivation behind your dream and work to rekindle your desire. Refer to the chapter entitled "It's Your Life" to gain a better understanding of your motivation for pursuing a particular dream.

BLACK AND WHITE THINKING

When we look at things as purely black and white or right and wrong we limit our problem solving options. We overlook grey areas that may be highly valuable. Grey areas may not solve the entire problem but they often provide a partial solution that keeps us moving forward.

PRIORITIES CHANGE

Has your dream lost its place of priority in your life? Sometimes we need to put a dream on hold because other things have become more important. That's just life. You'll need to decide if the time away from your dream is temporary or permanent.

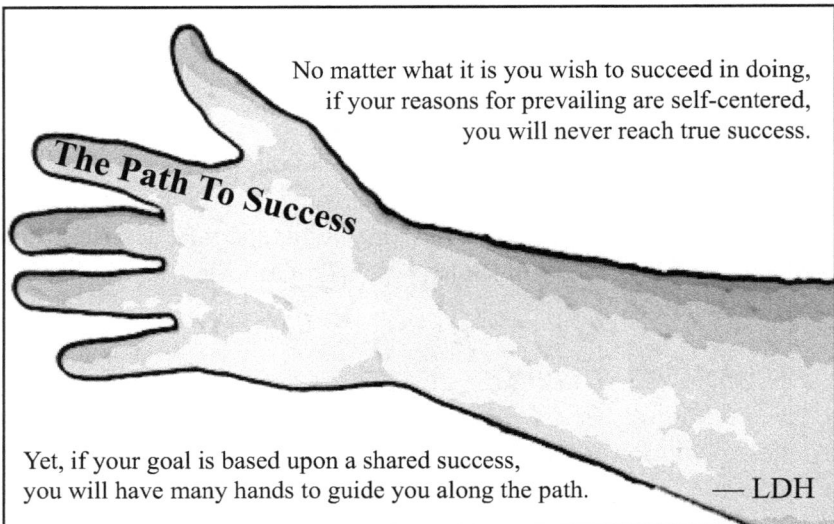

The Path To Success

No matter what it is you wish to succeed in doing, if your reasons for prevailing are self-centered, you will never reach true success.

Yet, if your goal is based upon a shared success, you will have many hands to guide you along the path.

— LDH

PUTTING A PEBBLE
IN YOUR OWN SHOE

Sometimes we do things, consciously or unconsciously, that sabotage our own success. Our self defeating behaviors (and we all have them) can cost us our dreams. It's as if we put a pebble in our own shoe that inhibits our progress toward our goals. This realization can knock the wind out of you. But once you recover, and begin to make changes, you will realize that the pain of such a discovery is well worth it. So start pulling the pebbles from your shoe and begin moving forward again toward your dreams.

Sometimes we have the dream
but we are not ourselves ready for the dream.
We have to grow to meet it.

— Louis L'Amour,
western fiction writer

GET TO KNOW YOUR GOPHERS

Photo: Please note, no gophers were hurt during the writing of this analogy.

There is an arcade game in which gophers pop up from many different holes in the ground. When you see a gopher you try to whack it on the head with a mallet. Hit one gopher and another one pops up. This is kind of the way it is when we try to stuff our emotions. An emotion pops up within us and we stuff it down rather than deal with it. This can be exhausting and stressful. When we drive our emotions underground, like gophers, they can do a lot of damage.

Thoughts give rise to emotions. Train yourself to think about what you are thinking about when you experience an undesirable feeling. A change in perspective will often change the feeling. If emotions stand in the way of your dreams you'll need to manage them better. Sooner or later you'll have to get to know your gophers, by getting in touch with your feelings.

Emotions have a powerful influence upon our life, and unless we control them, they will control us.

— Charles Stanley,
clergyman

ARE YOU STUCK IN THE MUCK?

Here are some tongue twisters to help understand why.

Are you BOGGED DOWN by bitterness, blame or a bad attitude?

Are you DELAYED due to difficulty, defensiveness or doubt?

Are you FROZEN by fear, fatigue or feelings of futility?

Are you HELD CAPTIVE by criticism or the fear of commitment?

Are you HINDERED by heartache, health issues or history?

Are you LIMITED by laziness, low self-esteem
or misplaced loyalty?

Are you MIRED in mediocrity, mistakes or emotion?

Are you PARALYZED by pride, poor planning or perfectionism?

Are you RESTRICTED by regrets or the fear of rejection?

Are you SHACKLED by stress, self-doubt
or self-defeating behaviors?

Or are you STUCK because you're passing the buck
and not taking full responsibility for your dreams?

Fix Your Leaks

How much time and money are you wasting that could be used toward your dream? In a notebook list your biggest waste of time and your biggest waste of money. Your friends and family may be able to help you identify some of your leaks. Decide if your dream is more important than these things and, if it is, make changes.

**Lost time
is never found again.**

— Benjamin Franklin

(Frankin was an author, printer, satirist, political theorist, politician, scientist, inventor, civic activist, statesman, soldier and diplomat.)

---

*It takes more courage to reveal insecurities
than to hide them,
more strength to relate to people
than to dominate them,
more 'manhood' to abide by thought-out principles
rather than blind reflex.
Toughness is in the soul and spirit,
not in muscles and an immature mind.*

—Alex Karras,
football player, wrestler and actor

Running... Out... Of... Gas

Even if you are passionate about your dream, you will never get to your goals if you keep running out of gas. With all the demands of everyday life, it's hard to have energy left over at the end of the day to put toward a dream. We must find ways to conserve and replenish your energy. Look at your routines, attitudes, associations, thoughts, habits, vices and so on. Ask yourself whether each of these is a boost to your energy, a drain or neutral. Your friends may be able to identify your leaks before you do. If you are serious about pursuing your dream, you will make the changes necessary to save energy for it.

CHECK YOUR BLIND SPOTS

Imagine you are driving in your car about to change lanes. You look around, everything looks clear, so you move over. Then wham! Out of nowhere you hit a car that was right there all along. You forgot to check your blind spots! We often avoid acknowledging our weaknesses by hiding behind our strengths. This is an accident waiting to happen. Is there an area of weakness in your life that is holding you back?

You may need to improve a skill, make a professional contact, get educated, break a bad habit, face a fear or learn how to better manage your resources or emotions. If a personal weakness is getting in the way of your dream you must acknowledge it and deal with it. It can be difficult to be objective about our blind spots, so turn to your support team for input.

Zip It... And Flip It

Many of us waste time and energy complaining about our circumstances. While we can't always change them, we can often choose our attitude. For example, we can choose to focus on the obstacle we face or the opportunity it presents. We can look at a problem through the eyes of fear or the eyes of faith. We can choose to be a worrier or a warrior. The following graphic illustrates how a flip in perspective, like the flip of a coin, may help us to see another side to an issue. This change often reveals unseen treasure. So, if you find yourself complaining about your circumstances, look for another perspective. In other words, zip it and flip it.

Obstacle	Opportunity	Fear	Faith
Adversity	Education	Get Bitter	Get Better
Wounds	Wisdom	Failure	Learning Experience
Stumbling Block	Stepping Stone	Victim	Survivor
Worrier	Warrior	Anxiety	Excitement
Wishing for it	Working at it	Finding Fault	Forgiveness

PAUSE & REFLECT

What can you learn from being stuck? Look for the lesson in this experience. It's helpful to describe your predicament in detail. Get your thoughts out of your head and onto paper. Look for patterns to your problems. Here are twenty questions to consider.

1. Has the fear of change got you in chains?
2. Are you defending your mistakes?
3. Are you waiting for things to happen?
4. Have you made poor choices that need to be rectified?
5. Are your emotions or attitudes holding you back?
6. Is fear of failure or success causing you to hesitate?
7. Have you closed your mind to possible solutions to problems?
8. Have you bitten off more than you can chew?
9. Are you distracted?
10. Are you knotted up with negativity?
11. Are you motivated enough to get unstuck?
12. Are you too overwhelmed or stressed out to get anything done?
13. Is it time to take a break and renew your energy?
14. Have you resisted seeking help?
15. Can you achieve your goals in the time you have allotted?
16. Have your values been compromised?
17. Have you veered off course or lost your compass?
18. Is there a leap of faith that you have been afraid to take?
19. Did you underestimate the impact of your dream on your life?
20. Has something else taken priority over your dream?

My ancestors
wandered in the wilderness
for 40 years
because even in biblical times,
men would not stop to ask for directions.

— Elayne Boosler,
comedian

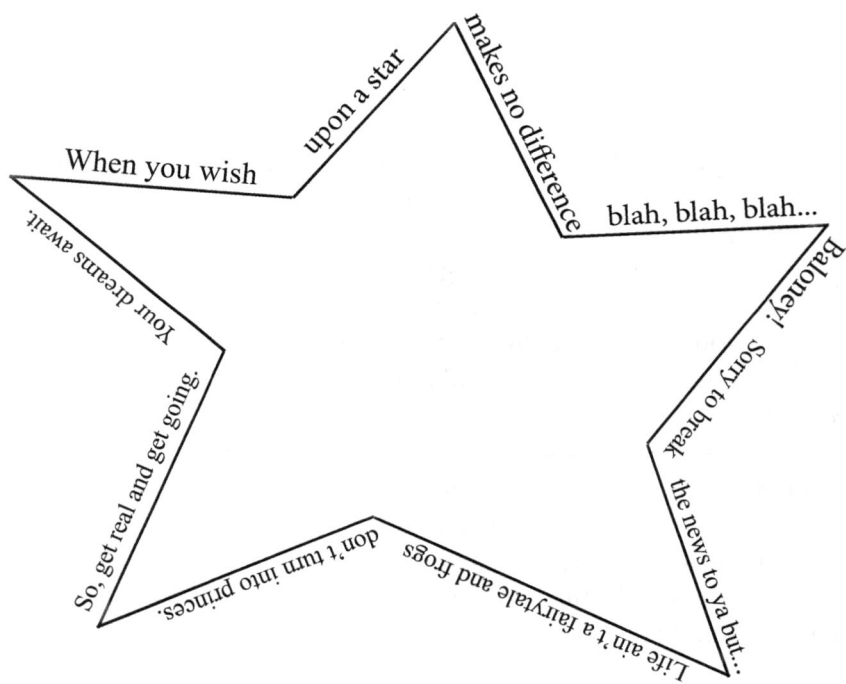

When you wish upon a star makes no difference blah, blah, blah... Baloney! Sorry to break the news to ya but... Life ain't a fairytale and frogs don't turn into princes. So, get real and get going. Your dreams await.

11

A WHOLE
MESS

O'
STRESS

I burn my candle at both ends,
It will not last the night.
But ah, my foes, and oh, my friends,
It gives a lovely light.

— Edna St. Vincent Millay,
poet and playwright

(The first woman to receive
the Pulitzer Prize for Poetry.)

FILL'ER UP
(a story about perspective)

Once there was a little boy
who pulled his wagon in the rain.
Collecting drops of rocket fuel,
he smiled as he skipped on his way. Singing . . .

Fill'er up. Fill'er up once more.
Carry me, give me wings so I can soar.
Fill'er up. Fill'er up for me. So I can live my dreams.

But when he grew, like men will do,
he forgot the magic of the rain.
In stormy times he counted clouds
as precious fuel rushed down the drain.

Perched on a barstool he ordered a shot
then said to himself,
"This is all I've got!"

REPEAT CHORUS

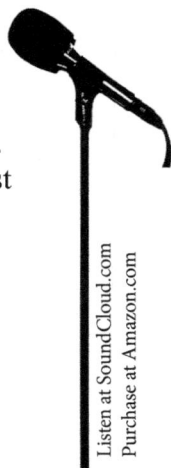

Leaving the tavern he dropped to his knees
and cried to the heavens, "What's happened to me?"

Then the wind arose
it seemed to whisper, "Welcome home."
A drop of rain caught his cheek and made him cry.
His mind flashed back to that moment from the past
when his heart could be refueled in stormy times.

Drenched with excitement he jumped to his feet
with arms open wide he flew down the street.
Singing . . .

REPEAT CHORUS

A WHOLE MESS O' STRESS

Tears are not the pain.
They are the healing.

— Dr. Annette Goodheart,
laughter coach

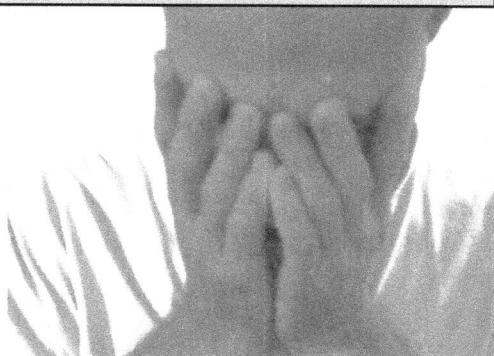

The pursuit of a difficult dream can be stressful. It's important to develop tools for coping with the stress of change, sacrifice, disappointment, criticism and even success. The more stress-management tools you have, the better your chances of addressing problems quickly and correctly. Below are some tools to assist. Be aware that "stressed out" can lead to "burned out". Burn out may be accompanied by apathy, loss of motivation, isolation and depression. If stress interferes with the quality of your life it's important to seek professional assistance.

ASSESS YOUR WORKLOAD

Are you trying to do too much? Take a look at your To Do List and prioritize the tasks. Postpone things that are not critical and adjust deadlines if they are unrealistic. If you are trying to do too many things at once, nothing gets done. It is helpful to describe the projects, responsibilities and commitments that you are currently juggling. For example, with regard to your career you may be working overtime, improving your computer skills and striving for a promotion. Your family goals may include: spending more time together, saving money for a vacation and saving to buy a home. The number of goals you are juggling can add up quickly. Decide where you need to focus your attention; then prioritize, eliminate, postpone or delegate. It's important to include fun things on your To Do List alongside your tasks. These activities will keep you motivated to work through the tough stuff so you can have some fun.

DO A STRESS SCAN

During stressful times it's helpful to check your stress level on a regular basis. Many wrist watches can be set to beep on the hour providing an easy reminder. Each time you hear the alarm, assess your level of stress. Check your posture. Are you hunched over? Check your breathing. Is it relaxed or labored? Are you grinding your teeth? Is your mind racing? Use the alarm as a reminder to consciously do a stress scan and implement a stress reduction strategy, if needed.

ACCEPT A LENDING HAND

For many of us, it is easier to lend a helping hand than to ask for one. During stressful times your support team becomes a great asset. Use them when you need friendly ear, a new perspective or an escape

UNLOAD BEFORE YOU EXPLODE

Doctors T.H. Holmes and R.H. Rahe developed a method for assessing a person's stress level. It's called *The Social Readjustment Ratings Scale*. This scale lists 41 stressful life events (both positive and negative) and assigns a numeric value to each event on a scale of 1 to 100. For example: the death of a spouse equals 100 points, a change in financial state equals 38 points and an outstanding personal achievement equals 28 points. Believe it or not, retirement is stressful enough for the average person to receive 45 out of 100 points. In times of stress, it's helpful to refer to this scale and make a list of the stressors you are dealing with at the moment. Your heightened awareness will enable you to decide if you are juggling too much and if some of the stressors can be eliminated or postponed. Pace yourself and find healthy stress releases.[1]

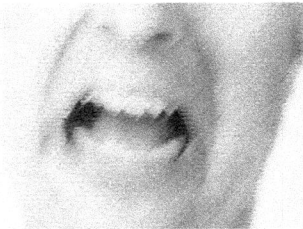

from the grind.

ADOPT A DIFFERENT ATTITUDE

Nobel Prize Nominee Hans Selye is known as the founder of the concept of stress. Selye recognized that, "Adopting the right attitude can convert a negative stress into a positive one."[2] Not all stress is bad. In fact, stress can be a great motivator which spurs us on to personal growth and achievement.

EXERCISE YOUR RIGHT TO BE LESS STRESSED

Exercise is a great stress release especially when you keep it fun. Choose something you enjoy like tennis, dancing or hiking and it won't feel like a workout. Yoga and Tai Chi are helpful because they incorporate specific techniques for stress reduction.

CHANGE WHAT'S NOT WORKING

Sometimes we keep pounding our head into the same wall over and over again trying to break through. This can be very stressful. It may be time to lift your head, take a step back and get some rest. Then look for a new pathway around the obstacle that is causing you stress. If you keep on doing the same thing over and over, how can you expect a different result?

CHECK YOUR ENVIRONMENT

A poor environment may be adding to your stress level. Insufficient lighting, distracting noises, poor air quality, clutter, an uncomfortable workspace and other environmental factors may exacerbate an already stressful situation. Look for ways to make improvements. Studies have

If you have a song of faith in your heart, it will be heard by the look on your face.

— Unknown

shown that colors can impact our mood. Cool colors such as green, blue, purple, grey and white can have a calming affect.[3] Consider filling the air with soothing sounds like soft music or white noise, and calming aromas like essential oils or scented candles.

WHAT'S EATING YOU

Poor dietary habits contribute to our level of stress; and stressful times often worsen poor eating habits. The Food and Mood Project, a nutrition research group in the United Kingdom, performed a study in which they separated foods into two categories: food stressors and food supporters. Food stressors are foods that have been found to intensify stress, while food supporters are foods that are helpful to people under stress. Participants in the study reported a significant improvement in their mental health when they made healthier food choices during stressful times. Examples of food stressors are: sugar, caffeine, alcohol and chocolate. Food supporters include: water, vegetables, fruit and oil-rich fish. Other helpful food-related stress reduction strategies include: eating meals on a regular schedule, carrying nutritious snacks and planning meals in advance.[4]

SAY HELLO... TO SOME H_2O

If you are not drinking enough water you can easily and unnecessarily drain your energy. For our bodies to function properly we must have adequate hydration. According to the National Federation of Professional Trainers, "at 2% dehydration, the body's work capacity decreases by 12-15%."[5] To get a general estimate of how much water you need to drink daily, take your weight in pounds and divide by two. This is the number of ounces of water you need daily. Don't deny yourself the fuel your body needs to pursue your dream.

HOCUS-POCUS CHANGE YOUR FOCUS

When the pursuit of your dream becomes stressful it's easy to fall into the trap of focusing on the things that aren't working. This tunnel vision can get us even more stressed. It's helpful to make a list of your accomplishments, things that you are excited about and the things and people in your life for which you are thankful. This simple act can be very uplifting. Like magic, many of your troubles will disappear in the light of healthier perspective and an attitude of gratitude.

GET SOME *ZZZZZZZZ*'S

The National Sleep Foundation (NSF) offers the following tips for a better night sleep. Maintain a regular bed time and wake time, even on the weekends. Establish a regular, relaxing bedtime routine (i.e. hot bath, relaxing music). Create a sleep-conducive environment. Sleep on a comfortable mattress and pillows. Finish eating at least 2-3 hours before your regular bedtime. Exercise regularly but complete your workout at least a few hours before bedtime. Avoid caffeine, nicotine and alcohol close to bedtime. Visit the NSF at: www.sleepfoundation. org for more information.[6]

LAUGH A LITTLE

Laughter is a great stress release. Dr. Joel Goodman advises, "Seven days without laughter makes one weak." Bill Cosby believes, "If you can find humor in anything, even poverty, you can survive it." A little laughter will lift your spirits when getting to your goals is difficult.

SCHEDULE TIME TO UNWIND
Many people enjoy gardening, nature walks, back rubs, reading, listening to music, painting, playing with a pet, bike riding, a hot bath, and so on. Schedule time to unwind.

START A STRESS DIARY

It may be helpful to take notes about what is causing you stress. A stress diary will assist you in identifying stress patterns, stress triggers and unhealthy responses to stress. A diary will also assist you in determining which stress reducing techniques work best for you. Be cautious, though. Writing about your problems may give them more power. Therefore, write about the solutions.

THE POWER OF PRAYER

One of my favorite stress releasers is the Serenity Prayer by Reinhold Niebuhr: "God grant me the serenity to accept the things I cannot change; courage to change the things I can; and wisdom to know the difference. Pursuing a difficult dream requires acceptance, courage and wisdom.

CRY, RANT AND RAVE

Comedienne Phyllis Diller has her own recipe for dealing with anger and frustration. She sets the kitchen timer for twenty minutes then cries, rants, and raves. At the sound of the bell she simmers down and goes about business as usual.

> Don't look past the treasures
> of your own adventures
> to the desert of another's expectations.
> For in the mirror of another's eye,
> the colors of the rainbow
> may not yet have been seen.
>
> — LDH

TAKE 2 FOR U

It is so important to take a couple of minutes during stressful times to give yourself a break and a chance to relax. When you do, you will feel better and be able to address your challenges with more clarity. I've created a two-minute instrumental song called, "Take 2 for U." It can be used to assist you in practicing meditation and relaxation techniques. I've included some examples to try. So the next time you feel stress start to build inside, remember to take 2 for U.

Abdominal Breathing

A simple technique for meditation is to bring your attention to your breath. While lying on your back place one hand on your belly and observe the rise and fall of the abdomen. Now select a pattern for your breathing. For example, breathe in over four seconds then out over four seconds. Whenever distracting thoughts enter your mind simply return your focus to the breath.

Mantra Meditation

In this form of meditation you repeat a word or phrase to yourself. It's helpful to make up affirmations related to your dream such as, "There are no limits to what I can achieve" or "I have the power to bring my dreams to life" or "I am confident I will overcome any obstacles I face." When distracting thoughts enter your mind return your attention to the mantra without judgement.

Visualization

When you use your imagination to picture a relaxing scene in your mind your body responds by relaxing. Use all of your senses to enhance the detail of the image. Whenever distracting thoughts pop into your mind simply return your mental focus to the relaxing scene. Here are a couple examples to try.

a.   Imagine you are at the beach. Listen to your breathing. Your exhalation sounds like a crashing wave, your inhalation sounds like the ocean drawing back into itself after a wave. Imagine the waves gently washing over you drawing the stress from your body and mind and replacing it with peace.

b.   In your mind picture a candle burning. Breathe in slowly. As you exhale imagine the candle gently flickering. Watch the candle and its response to your breathing.

Progressive Muscle Relaxation

When we get stressed we often hold tension in our muscles. This technique will help release the tension. While lying on your back focus your mind on the muscles of your feet. Tighten these muscles then relax them. Then work up your body one muscle group at a time to your calf muscles, thighs, buttocks, abdomen, back, chest, arms, hands, neck and face. Tighten and relax each part of your body several times then move on to the next area. Focus your mind on the sensation of tightness (tension) and release (relaxation). This exercise helps increase body awareness thus enabling you to sense tension as it builds and to make the choice to release it.

Photo: She's either very good or very gassy!

Let Your Mind Wander

With this form of meditation you let your mind wander and watch where it goes without judgment or analysis. It will give you insight into your predominant thoughts. Your mind may be prompting you to deal with an issue that needs resolution.

Moving Meditation

Tai Chi, Qi Gong and yoga are great forms of moving meditation. Another form that requires no training or expense is Walking Meditation. While you walk simply inhale for a designated number of steps, then exhale over a designated number of steps. With practice you will gain better control of your breathing and mental concentration. Vary the number of steps for a greater challenge.

LOST IN A SEA OF EMOTION

Pursuing a difficult dream can give rise to many emotions. Some can keep us from our dreams. I find it helpful to compare emotions to ocean waves. Both rise up, seemingly out of nowhere, and can take us for a ride. If an emotion is healthy, have fun and enjoy the journey. On the other hand, riding unhealthy waves of emotion wave can push us off course and be very damaging. The further you ride a negative wave the more powerful it becomes. Emotions are normal and natural. Learn from them, but don't let them drive your life or ruin your dreams. Recognize which emotional waves are healthy to ride and which ones will leave you, and your dreams, lost in a sea of emotion.

Photo: That's my lone paddle on the left.

Dreams Give Us Wings

In high school I was always the smallest kid in the class by a good bit, and was not especially coordinated, and certainly not the athlete type, who enjoyed running around outside, and was socially kind of immature, not the comfortable leader, teenager type. And so, when I began getting into model airplanes, and getting into contests and creating new things, I probably got more psychological benefit from that than I would have from some of the other typical school things.[7]

— Paul MacCready,
aeronautical engineer

(Inventor of the Gossamer Condor, the first practical
flying machine powered by a human being.)

It may be time to...

put your feet up
and relax.

LDH

A Mental Tug-O-War

Two teams line up on either side of a long rope. In the middle, a mud pit. You guessed it: a tug-o-war. Sometimes I feel like there's a tug-o-war going on in my mind; the winner gets control of my thinking. Some of my common battles are between doubt and faith, anger and forgiveness as well as self pity and confidence. This mental tug-o-war can be exhausting. I've discovered a strategy that I find helpful: Let go of the rope!

In your imagination, see the negative thoughts as your opponent in the tug-o-war. Remember, if negativity wins it pulls you away from your dreams. Now, let go of the rope and see your opponent go flying. Next, pick an activity that engages your mind in a positive way. By filling your mind with desired thoughts there is less room for negativity to creep in. I've found that the more I try to fight unwanted thoughts, the more power I give them. The more I try to shut them out, the louder they knock to get in. Remember, whatever controls your thinking controls your life. Don't let the pull of negative thinking drag you away from your dreams.

Dwelling on the negative simply contributes to its power.

— Shirley MacLaine,
actress, dancer, activist and author

Can You Guess What They Have in Common?

"Gone with the Wind"
by Margaret Mitchell (38 rejections)

"Chicken soup for the soul"
by Jack Canfield and Mark Victor Hansen
(140 rejections)

"Jonathan Livingston Seagull"
by Richard Bach (14 rejections)

"Zen and the Art of Motorcycle Maintenance"
by Robert Pirsig (121 rejections)

"Carrie"
by Stephen King (30 rejections)

"M*A*S*H"
by Richard Hooker (21 rejections)

— All were Best Sellers[8]

12

A Healthy Balance

DREAMS REALITY

SEEMS TO ME

Seems to me
rarely do we live as we once had dreamed.
Holding on to memories of what could be.
Seems to me seldom do we take
the time to believe
there could be some options
to the life we lead.

CHORUS:
Seems to me somewhere we get lost along the way.
Planning for the future, we lose sight of today.
Seems to me somehow we could find a way to live
where dreams and reality could co-exist.
Surely you'd admit we need a world like this.

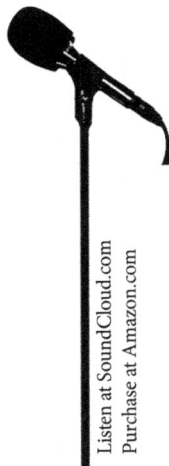

Seems to me if we take a look beyond what we see.
We would find a world inside with all we need.
Seems to me there will come a time
when people will see
the value of one's life is set internally.

REPEAT CHORUS

Sometimes I wonder why
there's not enough love in the world.
Man will search and man will find
whatever he calls his jewels.
Seem to me we spend our lives
reaching out for what lies within.
Maybe how we treat ourselves
is where honest love begins.

REPEAT CHORUS

We need a world like this.

A HEALTHY BALANCE

There are people who want to be
everywhere at once,
and they get nowhere.

— Carl Sandburg
(winner of two Pulitzer Prizes in Literature)

While Carl Friedrich Gauss, a German mathematician and Astronomer, was working he was interrupted and informed that his wife was dying. He is purported to have said, "Ask her to wait a moment — I am almost done." Dreams can be so enticing and so demanding that, if we're not careful, they can easily pull our lives out of balance and wreak havoc with our priorities. Be careful. Remember to set goals in every area of your life including: Career, Family, Finances, Social, Health (Physical, Mental and Spiritual), Education, Recreation, Charity, Creativity, etc. Keep in mind that success in some areas may come easier to you than other areas. A person may be highly successful in business but let his health or relationships slide. What good is a great career if you don't have your health or the time to enjoy the fruits of your labor?

STRIVING YET STARVING

Are you moving toward your dream yet feeling miserable? We can check off goal after goal on the way to our dream, yet never take time to enjoy the process, or celebrate our successes. It's important to ask yourself if you are striving for success, yet starving your spirit. We may make statements like, "I'll be happy when…" or "When I get there I'll have time to …." Be careful what you put off until tomorrow. Tomorrow may never come. If you can't find pleasure in the pursuit of this dream, it's okay to let it go and turn your attention to a different dream.

YOU ARE MORE THAN YOUR DREAM

There is an expression, "If you are what you do, when you don't you aren't." For many people retirement is the kiss of death because throughout their career they relied upon their work to provide their sense of identity and self-worth. It's easy to fall into this trap and define ourselves by our job, social status, appearance, financial means, or dream. If we cling too tightly to one of these identities, and lose it, we run the risk of losing ourselves in the process. If you are your dream, who will you be without it? The hard reality is: many difficult dreams do not come true. Seek a path that enables you to be happy, healthy and fulfilled as you pursue your dream; no matter what the outcome. A dream is only a part of who you are. If you are relying upon the success of a particular dream for your self worth, happiness or fulfillment, it could be a recipe for disaster.

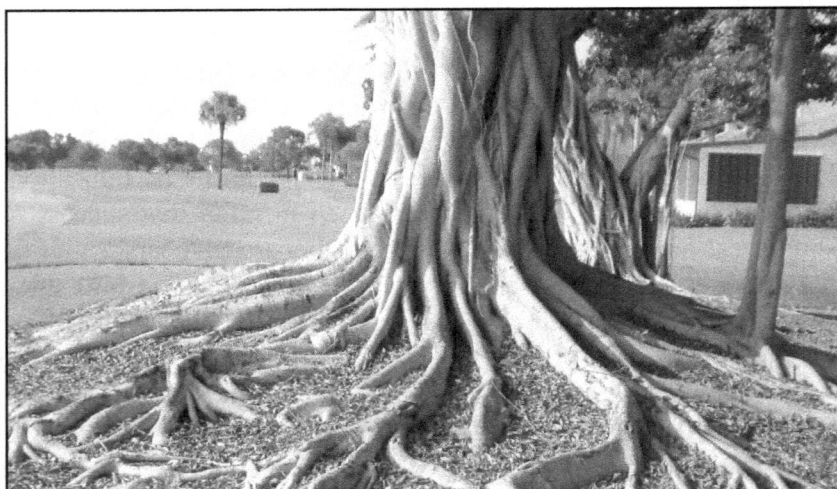

Don't ever forget your roots.
The tallest and broadest of trees
topple in the slightest of breezes
if its roots have been starved
in the quest to stand out amongst the forest.

— LDH

ARE YOU JUGGLING TOO MUCH?

As people in pursuit of a difficult dream there is much to be learned from jugglers. It is difficult enough to juggle career, family, finances, health and so on. Toss in a dream and it can become overwhelming. If one club gets all of your attention, the rest come tumbling down.

We must learn to recognize our limits, yet strive to expand the possibilities. We must acknowledge that we will be forever growing and adapting as we strive to maintain balance. We must learn to identify when we are overextending ourselves and to say "no" to some things, even good things, until they fit more effectively into the overall balance. Some dreams may need to wait until they can be pursued in a healthy manner. In the meantime, choose another dream.

Photo: I cheated on this photo. I can juggle three clubs but Photoshop helped me with the other two... I'm still dreaming about five though.

WHEN A STRENGTH BECOMES A WEAKNESS

*The characteristics that make you successful
are the very same traits
that can cause your failure.*

—Robert J. Fierle,
entrepreneur

I believe that one of my strengths is my imagination. This helps me creatively, but can become a problem when my imagination runs wild. Take a look at what you consider to be your strengths. Be aware that a strength that is out of balance may become a weakness that derails your dreams. Below are some examples.

- The kind person who becomes a doormat
- The analytical thinker who analyzes everything
- The man who can "do it all" but burns out because he won't delegate
- The great businessman who is a stranger at home
- The great multi-tasker who takes on too much
- The man with a zillion ideas but nothing completed
- The self-reliant man who refuses to ask for help
- The problem solver who invents problems to solve
- The risk taker who is hooked on the adrenaline rush
- The man who handles change well but gets board when things become routine
- The technical wizard who can't relate to people
- The doer who can't stop doing and just relax
- The intellectual who hasn't learned to trust his gut
- The caring person who cares for others yet neglects his or her own needs

THROWING DARTS

Going after a dream is like throwing a dart at a dartboard — the tougher the dream, the tougher the shot. Some dreams are so difficult they are comparable to trying to hit a bulls-eye from fifty yards away. The odds of doing it are low but it could be done. Sure, go ahead and throw that dart, but also consider variations on your dream with better odds for success. At times, we get so focused on trying to hit the jackpot that we overlook other dreams that would be just as fulfilling. As you pursue your dreams look for ways to improve your chances for success.

Aim high at a high mark and you will hit it.
No, not the first time, nor the second,
and maybe not the third.
But keep on aiming and keep on shooting.
For only practice will make you perfect.
Finally you'll hit the bulls-eye of success.

— Annie Oakley,
sharpshooter

BEFORE THEIR DREAMS CAME TRUE

Match the celebrity
to a previously held job.[1]

1.	___ Jennifer Aniston	a.	Amusement ride operator
2.	___ Madeleine Albright	b.	Bartender
3.	___ Dan Aykroyd	c.	Bouncer
4.	___ Alec Baldwin	d.	Bricklayer
5.	___ Marlon Brando	e.	Coal miner
6.	___ Charles Bronson	f.	Computer programmer
7.	___ Sandra Bullock	g.	Dept. store bra sales
8.	___ Sean Connery	h.	Ditch digger
9.	___ Elvis Costello	i.	Gas station attendant
10.	___ Danny DeVito	j.	Hair stylist
11.	___ Michael Douglas	k.	Clown
12.	___ Clint Eastwood	l.	Pool installer
13.	___ Whoopi Goldberg	m.	Coffin polisher
14.	___ Howie Mandel	n.	Postal service
15.	___ Ozzy Osbourne	o.	Slaughterhouse worker
16.	___ Sylvester Stallone	p.	Telemarketer/waitress
17.	___ Hugh Jackman	q.	Deli counter attendant
18.	___ Ellen DeGeneres	r.	Paralegal
19.	___ Aston Kutcher	s.	Singing telegrams
20.	___ Nathan Lane	t.	Cereal plant worker
21.	___ Cyndi Lauper	u.	Horse walker
22.	___ Ralph Lauren	v.	Telemarketing (pens)
23.	___ Johnny Depp	w.	Retail sweater sales
24.	___ Lucy Liu	x.	Aerobics instructor

Answer Key:

1-p, 2-g, 3-n, 4-c, 5-h, 6-e, 7-b, 8-m, 9-f, 10-j, 11-i, 12-l, 13-d, 14-a, 15-o, 16-q, 17-k, 18-r, 19-t, 20-s, 21-u, 22-w, 23-v, 24-x

13

WALK WITH DETERMINATION

The most powerful weapon on earth is the human soul on fire.

— Ferdinand Foch, soldier and military theorist

KEEP OUR DREAMS ALIVE

SECTION 1:
Nothin' will change unless we make it,
won't change till we try.
We can't make the world surrender,
gotta keep our dreams alive.

Everyone has a dream. We possess the power
to live the life we believe will build our victory tower.

CHORUS:
Nothin' ventured, nothin' gained, the whole world stays the same.
Take a chance you'll be amazed, the power that you have.

REPEAT SECTION 1
Keep our dreams alive. Keep our dreams alive.

Once we recognize the past is over, we can learn to live today.
Livin' it again won't make it better.
There's no way the past can change.

All that we really need
to make life a celebration
is to choose the path of a dream
and walk with determination.

REPEAT CHORUS

All that we really need to make life a celebration
is to choose the path of a dream
and walk with determination.

REPEAT CHORUS & SECTION 1

Keep our dreams alive. (Repeat to end)

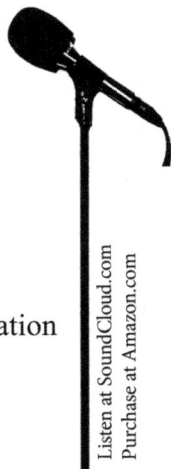

WALK WITH DETERMINATION

*Character consists of what you do
on the third and fourth tries.*

— James Michener,
Pulitzer Prize Winner for Fiction

Charles Best dreamed of being a public school teacher since he was in high school. When he was hired to teach social studies in the Bronx, he quickly learned a harsh reality about the public school system — there aren't enough supplies, books and other tools available for teachers to do their jobs effectively. He noticed that many teachers were forced to spend their own money just to get by. In frustration, Best may have given up on his dream, but instead he looked for a way to resolve the problem. He believed that many people would make donations to schools if they had more control over how their contributions were spent. This led to the creation of DonorsChoose. org, a website where teachers submit requests and donors choose which projects to fund. If you believe you are destined to pursue a dream, remember: destiny is a matter of choice not chance.[1]

KEEP ON TRYING
No matter what happens give yourself credit for trying; and keep on trying. A setback or failure can be a blessing. It can open your eyes to areas where you are weak or need to work smarter. Take full responsibility for your life and your dreams; and learn from every experience.

A DOUBLE-EDGED DREAM
When talking with people who are driven by a difficult dream, some view their passion as both a blessing and a curse. On the one hand, they are driven to reach their goals, yet all too often life gets in the way.

Some have said, in frustration, that it would have been easier if they were deaf to the call of their dream and could just follow the crowd. Only you can decide which of your dreams are worth pursuing. Not every dream will come true. If you can't find pleasure in the pursuit of this dream, regardless of the outcome, pick another dream.

CHIP AWAY AT YOUR GOAL

When I first walked into a martial arts school I was amazed by the complexity of the movements that the advanced students were doing. I felt excited, but at the same time, overwhelmed and intimidated. I thought I could never do what they were doing. My instructor taught me that everything which appears complex can be broken down into a series of simpler components. By learning each component individually, I could eventually assemble various pieces together and achieve things that I never believed possible. Keep chipping away at the smaller goals that will lead you to your dreams.

OVERWHELMED BY THE BIG PICTURE

Some dreams are more complex than others and therefore require a greater number of steps. It's important to look at the "big picture" and get a realistic view of what it will take to reach your goal. With any difficult dream there will be times when the enormity of the challenge seems overwhelming. We must remember to focus on the task at hand and take the next step.

Don't cross the bridge before you come to it.
— Anonymous

THEY DREAMED AN IMPOSSIBLE DREAM

- Bill Lear (Lear Jet)
- Erik Weihenmayer (first blind person to scale Mt. Everest)
- Fred Smith (Federal Express)
- Gustave Leven (Perrier Bottled Water Company)
- King Camp Gillette (An affordable disposable razor)
- Mike Powell (Broke Bob Beamon's long jump record)
- Orville and Wilbur Wright (heavier-than-air flying machine)
- Roger Bannister (to run a sub-four-minute mile)
- Ted Turner (to create CNN – an all-news network)
- Spencer Silver (3-M "Post-It" Notepads)
- Henry Ford (the motorcar)
- Robert Goddard (rocket propulsion in outer space)
- Margaret Thatcher (a female British Prime Minister)
- Arthur Jones (Nautilus Exercise equipment)
- Estee Lauder (considered foolhardy for offering free cosmetic samples)
- Mrs. Fields (cookie stores)
- Helen Keller (first deafblind person to earn a Bachelor of Arts degree)

Missing a few limbs doesn't stop me from doing the thing I love most.

— Cornel Hrisca-Munn,
drummer

Note: Cornel Hrisca-Munn made it to the United Kingdom's Young Drummer of the Year Finals in 2007 despite the fact that he has no lower arms and has had one leg amputated.[2]

Faith In Action

In a survey taken by Success Magazine people were asked what they believed to be the single most important element for success. 41 percent said Faith, followed by Family (25.5 percent), a Balanced Life (11.7 percent) and Happiness (7.3 percent). Faith comes in many forms — faith in ourselves, others and in a higher power. I've heard it said that God gives us our dreams. If you believe this to be true, it doesn't excuse you from doing the work, developing the skills and implementing the plan necessary to achieve your dream. Faith and action are required.[3]

Pray as if everything depended on God,
and work as if everything depended on man.

— Cardinal Francis Spellman

Look familiar?

This is you watching other people live their dreams. From here you don't have a remote chance of living your own.

LDH

FROM TROUBLE TO TRIUMPH

I was exhausted and demoralized, and said to myself, "Well, I guess second place isn't too bad." But then through the blur of fatigue, I remembered the vision of myself winning the 1986 Iditarod, and I knew this race could be mine alone. And so for the next forty-four miles, I ran, pumped with one leg or pushed until I passed Joe and won my first Iditarod.[4]

— Susan Butcher,
Dog-Sled Racer

Why do I see things differently from the way other people see them? Why do I pursue the questions that I pursue, even if others regard them as, as they say, "controversial?" Which merely means that they have a difference of opinion. They see things differently. I am interested both in nature and in the human side of nature, and how the two can be brought together, and effective in a useful way.[5]

— Jonas Salk,
Developer of Polio Vaccine

There was no reason for me to believe I could be a successful writer....Yet, deep inside, I had always felt a need to tell stories. Up until that point, it was a dream I had never allowed myself to consider. Now, at thirty-five, I was whispering that dream to myself. But with that whisper came constant thoughts of negativity and self doubt. Despite my fear, I quit my job and began to write.[6]

— Olivia Goldsmith,
Author of the First Wives Club

Mountain of Success

Enter any new situation
with the assumption that,
no matter what the outcome,
the knowledge gained
and the options explored toward new horizons,
will make you a stronger person.

Do not fear that to which you are unfamiliar;
for your assumptions are based upon your insecurities.
Rest your assumptions
upon the solid base of your accomplishments
and build a mountain of success.

— LDH

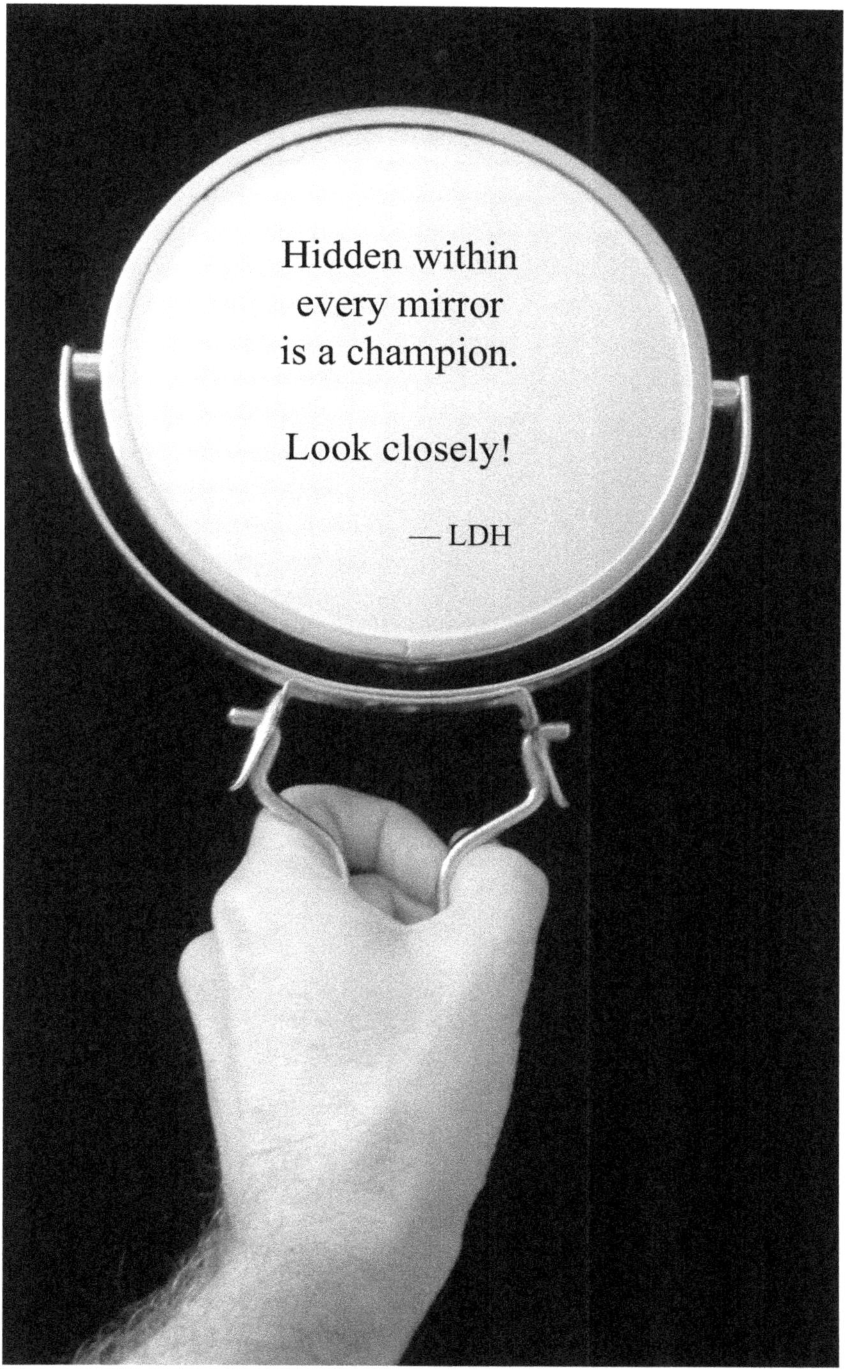
Hidden within
every mirror
is a champion.
Look closely!
— LDH

Tomorrow's Heroes

REFERENCES

Chapter 1:   **A Rumble Deep Inside**

1. About Mrs. Fields. (2009). Retrieved from http://debbifields.com/about. html

Chapter 2:   **It's Your Life**

1. Gore, A. (2007, August). *Al Gore - Nobel Lecture*. Retrieved from http://www.nobelprize.org/nobel_prizes/peace/laureates/2007/gore-lecture_en.html
2. Foster to Famous. (2010). *FosterClub*. Retrieved from http://www.fosterclub.com/famous
3. Famous Well Known People with Hearing Impairments and Deafness. (2008, Feb 18). *Disabled World*. Retrieved from http://www.disabled-world.com/artman/publish/famous-deaf.shtml
4. Famous People with the Gift of Dyslexia. (2009, Dec 1). Retrieved from http://www.dyslexia.com/famous.htm
5. Inskeep, S. (2007, Dec 26). Does Dyslexia Translate to Business Success? [Interview with Dr. Julie Logan]. *NPR Morning Edition*. Retrieved from http://www.npr.org/templates/story/story.php?storyId=17611066
6. Faces of Asthma. (2007). *Breath of Life. U.S. Nat'l Library of Medicine.* Retrieved from http://www.nlm.nih.gov/hmd/breath/Faces_asthma/facesframe.html
7. Robert Joffrey. (2009). *New World Encyclopedia.* Retrieved from http://www.newworldencyclopedia.org/entry/Robert_Joffrey
8. Famous People with Tourettes Syndrome. (2008, Jan 14). DisabledWorld.com. Retrieved from http://www.disabled-world.com/artman/publish/tourettes-famous.shtml
9. Bane, C. (2010). Jeremy Stenberg: Fan favorite. Retrieved from http://espn.go.com/action/fmx/blog/_/post/5906317/fan-favorite
10. Wade, L. (2009, July 27). At Camp Twitch and Shout, Tourette kids can be themselves. Retrieved from http://www.cnn.com/2009/HEALTH/07/27/tourette.camp/index.html
11. Famous People with Cerebral Palsy. (2008, Jan 17). Disabled World. Retrieved from http://www.disabled-world.com/artman/publish/cp-famous.shtml
12. Horsburgh, S. (2002, July 22). Life of a Salesman. *People*. Retrieved from http://www.people.com/people/archive/article/0,,20137570,00.html
13. Robinson, G. D. (2012). *With Great Power*. Retrieved from http://www.preaching.com/sermons/11548369/
14. Pageant Is Her Crowning Achievement. (2008, April 10). *CBS Interactive*.

Retrieved from http://www.cbsnews.com/stories/2008/04/10/entertainment/main4006779.shtml

15. Santana's Lifelong Struggle. (2008, Oct 23). *The Week.* Retrieved from http://www.theweek.com/article/index/90083/Santanas_lifelong_struggle

16. *Coles: I am a survivor of sexual abuse. (2005, Sep 19).* ESPN.com News Services. *Retrieved from http://sports.espn.go.com/nfl/news/story?id=2165781*

17. Elizabeth Fry, E. (2012). *A Childhood Biography of Oprah Winfrey.* Retrieved from http://oprah.about.com/od/oprahbiography/p/oprahchildhood.htm

18. *'Housewives' star Hatcher reveals sex abuse. (2006, Mar 8).* Associated Press. Retrieved from http://www.msnbc.msn.com/id/11717426/

19. Tori Amos. (2012). Retrieved from http://www.rollingstone.com/music/artists/tori-amos/biography Meyer, J. (2009). *Abuse and the Miracle of Recovery. Joyce Meyer Ministries.* Retrieved from http://www.joycemeyer.org/OurMinistries/EverydayAnswers/Articles/art51.htm

20. You can find a way to heal. (2007, Jan 23). *Parade.* Retrieved from http://www.parade.com/articles/editions/2007/edition_02-04-2007/Mary_J._Blige

21. Well-Known Adopted Persons, Birth Parents & Adoptive Parents. (2007). *Adoption Media.* Retrieved from http://celebrities.adoption.com/

22. Mulry, S, Connors, T, and Trecroci, D. (2008, Dec 17). Famous People With Diabetes. *Diabetes Health.* Retrieved from http://www.diabeteshealth.com/read/2008/12/17/5681/famous-people-with-diabetes/

23. Celebrity Stories of Bullying. (2007). *B-Free Alberta Children's Services.* Retrieved from http://www.b-free.ca/stories_good_company.html

24. Bullies: Who's A Target? (2005). *CastleWorks.* Retrieved from http://pbskids.org/itsmylife/friends/bullies/article3.html

25. Did You Know? (2009). *Surviving Bullies Project.* Weston, CT: Willoughby & Lamont Publishing. Retrieved from http://survivingbullies.com/index.php/resources/topic/category/didyouknow/

26. List of polio survivors. (2009). Retrieved from http://www.bionity.com/lexikon/e/List_of_polio_survivors/#_note-48/

27. Famous People with Speech Differences and Stutter. (2008). *DisabledWorld.com.* Retrieved from http://www.disabled-world.com/artman/publish/speech-famous.shtml

28. Holland, K. (2009). Celebrities With Attention Deficit Hyperactivity Disorder. *Health.com.* Retrieved from http://health.msn.com/health-topics/adhd/articlepage.aspx?cp-documentid=100251011

29. Bailey, E. (2009). Celebrities with ADHD. Retrieved from http://www.healthcentral.com/adhd/understanding-adhd-161681-5.html

30. Simon, G. (1999). How I Overcame Shyness. New York: Simon & Schuster.

31. Dara Torres Biography. (2010). Retrieved from http://daratorres.com/bio.php

32. Rodney Dangerfield. (2000). *Associated Press.* Retrieved from http://www.

legacy.com/Obituaries.asp?Page=LifeStory&PersonId=2679009

33. George Foreman Biography. (2010). *Biography.* Retrieved from http://www.biography.com/articles/George-Foreman-9298881

34. Mary Kay Ash Biography. (2010). *Biography.* Retrieved from http://www.biography.com/articles/Mary-Kay-Ash-19704

35. Van Ekeren, Glenn. (1994). *Speakers Sourcebook II.* Englewood Cliffs, NJ: Prentice Hall, p. 35.

36. Clara Barton: Founder of the American Red Cross. (2010). Retrieved from http://www.redcross.org/museum/history/claraBarton.asp

37. Van Ekeren, Glenn. (1994). *Speakers Sourcebook II.* Englewood Cliffs, NJ: Prentice Hall, p. 36.

38. Harlan Sanders Café and Museum - The World's First Kentucky Fried Chicken. (2010). Retrieved from http://www.corbinkentucky.us/sanderscafe.htm

39. Perez, A. J. (2006, May 24). Car owner Newman driving toward sunset. *USA Today.* Retrieved from http://www.usatoday.com/sports/motor/champ/2006-05-24-newman_x.htm

40. Grandma Moses Biography. (2012). *Encyclopedia of World Biography.* Retrieved from http://www.notablebiographies.com/Mo-Ni/Moses-Grandma.html

41. NASA's pioneering astronauts: Where are they now? (2012, August 25). *Associated Press.* Retrieved from http://www.usnews.com/science/news/articles/2012/08/25/nasas-pioneering-astronauts-where-are-they-now

42. Academy Awards Youngest and Oldest. (2010). *Suite101.* Retrieved from http://classicfilms.suite101.com/article.cfm/academy_awards_youngest_and_oldest

43. Mary Baker Eddy. (2010). *The Mary Baker Eddy Library.* Retrieved from http://www.marybakereddylibrary.org/mary-baker-eddy/life

44. Woman, 95, set to be oldest college graduate. (2007, Apr 27). *MSNBC.* Retrieved from http://www.msnbc.msn.com/id/18338864/

45. CNN Morning News. (2007, Apr 7). *CNN.* Retrieved from http://transcripts.cnn.com/TRANSCRIPTS/0704/07/smn.02.html

46. Ludwig Beethoven. (2012). *Biography.com.* Retrieved from http://www.biography.com/people/ludwig-van-beethoven-9204862

47. Thomas Edison. (2009). *Conservapedia.* Retrieved from http://www.conservapedia.com/Thomas_Edison

48. Chadwick, P. (2003). Famous (and not-so-famous) People with Disabilities. *Disability Social History Project.* Retrieved from http://www.disabilityhistory.org/people.html#powell

49. Apelo, C. P. (2008). Shaun White - Professional Snowboarder. *ABC of Snowboarding.* Retrieved from http://www.abc-of-snowboarding.com/info/shaun-white.asp

50. *Boxer, S. (2000, Feb 14). Charles M. Schulz, 'Peanuts' Creator, Dies at 77.* New York Times. *Retrieved from http://www.nytimes.com/learning/general/onthisday/bday/1126.html*

51. Overall Baseball Leaders and Baseball Records. (2009). Retrieved from http://www.baseball-reference.com/leaders/
52. Schwartz, L. (2007). Michael Jordan transcends hoops. ESPN.com. Retrieved from http://espn.go.com/sportscentury/features/00016048.html
53. Bob Cousy. (2009). *Encyclopedia.com*. Retrieved from http://www.encyclopedia.com/doc/1G2-3404707767.html
54. Larry King Live Weekend-Matt Lauer: Interview Highlights. (2001, Apr 1). CNN.com. Retrieved from http://transcripts.cnn.com/TRANSCRIPTS/0104/01/lklw.00.html
55. R.H. Macy & Co., Inc. History. (2012) Retrieved from http://www.fundinguniverse.com/company-histories/r-h-macy-co-inc-history/

Chapter 3:   That First Step

1. Young, Steve. (2002). *Great Failures of the Extremely Successful*. Los Angeles, CA: Tallfellow Press, p. 38.
2. Donald C. Johansen. (2010). *Academy of Achievement*. Retrieved from http://www.achievement.org/autodoc/page/joh1int-2
3. Glennon, L. (Ed.). (1998). *100 Most Important Women of the 20th Century*. Des Moines, Iowa: Ladies Home Journal Books, p. 7.
4. Glass, A. (2008, Sept 30). *First Hispanic American to serve in Congress, Sept. 30, 1822*. Retrieved from http://www.politico.com/news/stories/0908/14081.html
5. Glennon, L. (Ed.). (1998). *100 Most Important Women of the 20th Century*. Des Moines, Iowa: Ladies Home Journal Books, p. 7.
6. Edmonson, C. M. (1999). *Extraordinary Women*. Holbrook, MA: Adams Media Corporation.
7. Glennon, L. (Ed.). (1998). *100 Most Important Women of the 20th Century*. Des Moines, Iowa: Ladies Home Journal Books, p. 7.
8. Edmonson, C. M. (1999). *Extraordinary Women*. Holbrook, MA: Adams Media Corporation.
9. Glennon, L. (Ed.). (1998). *100 Most Important Women of the 20th Century*. Des Moines, Iowa: Ladies Home Journal Books, p. 60.
10. Jackie Robinson. (2012). *Biography.com*. Retrieved from http://www.biography.com/people/jackie-robinson-9460813
11. Glennon, L. (Ed.). (1998). *100 Most Important Women of the 20th Century*. Des Moines, Iowa: Ladies Home Journal Books, p. 39.
12. Thurgood Marshall. (2012). *Biography.com*. Retrieved from http://www.biography.com/people/thurgood-marshall-9400241
13. Schwartz, L. (2007). *Billie Jean Won For All Women*. Retrieved from http://espn.go.com/sportscentury/features/00016060.html
14. Drape, J. (2009, Sept 18). Earning Her Stripes in College Football. *The New York Times*. Retrieved from http://www.nytimes.com/2009/09/19/sports/ncaafootball/19ref.html

Chapter 4:   Someone To Cling To

Chapter 5:   Getting To Your Goals

1. Career Information - Actors, Producers, and Directors. (2010). *College Grad*. Retrieved from http://www.collegegrad.com/careers/proft23.shtml
2. Barnes, Brooks. (2008, June 30). Don't Forget the Middle People. *New York Times*. Retrieved from www.nytimes.com/2008/06/30/business/media/30strike.html
3. Bureau of Labor Statistics. (2010). Occupational Outlook Handbook, 2010-11 Edition - Actors, Producers, and Directors. *United States Department of Labor*. Retrieved from http://www.bls.gov/oco/ocos093.htm
4. Willingham, V. (2008, Nov 17). Half of primary-care doctors in survey would leave medicine. *CNN Health*. Retrieved from http://www.cnn.com/2008/HEALTH/11/17/ primary.care.doctors.study/index.html
5. Bureau of Labor Statistics. (2010). Occupational Outlook Handbook, 2010-11 Edition - Athletes, Coaches, Umpires, and Related Workers. *United States Department of Labor*. Retrieved from http://www.bls.gov/oco/ocos251.htm
6. How Songwriters Are Paid and the Federal Government's Role. (2010). *Nashville Songwriters Association International*. Retrieved from http://legislative.nashvillesongwriters.com/news.php?viewStory=76
7. General Minor League information. (2009). *Minor League Baseball*. Retrieved from http://web.minorleaguebaseball.com/milb/info/faq.jsp?mc=milb_info
8. What is the percent of college athletes make it professionally? (2009). Retrieved from http://wiki.answers.com/Q/What_is_the_percent_of_college_athletes_make_it_professionally
9. Tinsman, B. (2008). *The Game Inventor's Guidebook*. New York: Morgan James Publishing.
10. Young, Steve. (2002). *Great Failures of the Extremely Successful*. Los Angeles, CA: Tallfellow Press, p. 997.
11. Daniel Goldin. (2010). *Academy of Achievement*. Retrieved from Retrieved from http://www.achievement.org/autodoc/page/gol1int-1
12. Reeves, A. (2002, Jan 10). His Dedication And Long-Term View Saved Millions. *Investor's Business Daily*, p. A3.

Chapter 6:   Sharks In The Water

1. Heffernan, Lou. (2003). *An Ounce of Prevention: Simple Self Defense Strategies*. Jupiter, FL: Heffernan Publishing.
2. Majoras, D. P. (2009). The FTC in 2008: A Force for Consumers and Competition. *Federal Trade Commission*. Retrieved from www.ftc.gov/os/2008/03/ChairmansReport2008.pdf
3. 900 Numbers: FTC Rule Helps Consumers. (2009, Apr 24). *Federal Trade*

Commission. Retrieved from http://www.ftc.gov/bcp/edu/pubs/consumer/telemarketing/tel04.shtm

4. Kersey, Cynthia. (2005). *Unstoppable.* Naperville, IL: Sourcebooks, p. 292.

Chapter 7: **Putting Up With Put Downs**

1. Robert Fulton. (2009). Retrieved from http://www.statemaster.com/encyclopedia/Robert-Fulton
2. Weihenmayer, Erik. (2009). About Erik Weihenmayer World Class Adventurer. Retrieved from http://www.touchthetop.com/about.htm
3. Cerf, C. and Navasky, V. (1998). *The Experts Speak : The Definitive Compendium of Authoritative Misinformation.* New York: Random House, p. 228.
4. Contemporary Reviews - *Leaves of Grass* (1855). (2009). *The Walt Whitman Archive.* Retrieved from http://www.whitmanarchive.org/criticism/reviews/leaves1855/anc.00024.html
5. Sylvia Earle Undersea Explorer. (2009). *Academy of Achievement.* Retrieved from http://www.achievement.org/autodoc/steps/per?index=26
6. Cussler, C. and Dirgo, C. (1998). *Clive Cussler and Dirk Pitt Revealed.* New York: Simon & Schuster, p. 61.
7. Willem Kolff. (2010). *Academy of Achievement.* Retrieved from http://www.achievement.org/autodoc/page/kol0int-3
8. Cole, T. (2009, Aug 13). Guitar Legend And Innovator Les Paul Dies. *NPR Music.* Retrieved from http://www.npr.org/templates/story/story.php?storyId=111845182
9. Graham, T. (2009, June 4). Pre-Grilling, Foreman earned Hall of Fame. *ESPN.com.* Retrieved from http://a.espncdn.com/boxing/columns/graham_tim/1562912.html
10. Germ theory of disease. (2010). *Wikipedia.* Retrieved from http://en.wikipedia.org/wiki/Germ_theory_of_disease
11. Tinsman, B. (2008). *The Game Inventors Guide Book.* New York: Morgan James Publishing, p. 68.

Chapter 8: **Watch Your Thoughts**

1. Arntz, W. and Chasse, B. (Producers) & Vincente. M., Chasse, B. and Arntz, W. (Directors). (2004). *What the Bleep Do We Know?* United States: Lord of the Wind Film.
2. Donnelley, P. (2005). *Fade To Black: A Book Of Movie Obituaries, 2nd Edition.* London, UK, Omnibus Press, p. 173.
3. Bellis, M. (2009). Lewis Waterman. Retrieved from http://inventors.about.com/library/inventors/blwaterman.htm
4. Lambrecht, R.E. (2006, Spring). A Wisconsin Legend Ole Evenrude and His Outboard Motor. *Wisconsin Magazine of History.* Retrieved from

www.wisconsinhistory.org/wmh/pdf/spring06_lambrecht.pdf

5. James V. Kimsey, Founder of AOL. (1998, May 22). *Academy of Achievement*. Retrieved from http://www.achievement.org/autodoc/page/kim0int-1

6. For Dilbert's Scott Adams, It's All Work, All Play" by Curt Schleier. *Investor's Business Daily*, p. A3.

Chapter 9: Dare To Persevere

1. Kantrowitz, Barbara. (2003, July 28). A Writer Who Beat the Odds: Hillenbrand battled chronic fatigue to pen a best seller. *Newsweek*. Retrieved from http://www.encyclopedia.com/doc/1G1-105659831.html

2. Bellis, Mary. (2007, Sept 3). The History of Pez. *About, Inc.* Retrieved from http://inventors.about.com/od/foodrelatedinventions/a/pez_candy.htm

3. Bellis, Mary. (2007). Lillian Moller Gilbreth. *About, Inc.* Retrieved from http://inventors.about.com/library/inventors/blGilbreth.htm

4. All About Dr. Seuss. (2004). *Dr. Seuss Enterprises*. Retrieved from http://www.catinthehat.org/history.htm

5. Robbins, A. (1997). *Unlimited Power*. New York: Fireside.

6. Cerf, C. and Navasky, V. (1998). *The Experts Speak: The Definitive Compendium of Authoritative Misinformation*. New York: Random House.

7. Collins, B. (1969, Sept 1). Davis Cup? Oh, Get Stan Smith To Take Care Of That Chore. *Sports Illustrated*. Retrieved from http://sportsillustrated.cnn.com/vault/article/magazine/MAG1082776/2/index.htm

8. Institute of Electrical and Electronics Engineers. (2008). Vote Recording Machines. *IEEE*. Retrieved from http://www.ieeeghn.org/wiki/index.php/Vote_Recording_Machines

9. Gundersen, E. (2012). 50 years later, we're still mad for The Beatles. *USA Today*. Retrieved from http://www.usatoday.com/life/music/news/story/2012-06-10/beatles-50th-anniversary/55506324/1

10. King Camp Gillette. (2007). *Inventors Hall of Fame*. Retrieved from http://www.invent.org/Hall_Of_Fame/334.html

11. About Tiffany and Co. (2009). Retrieved from http://press.tiffany.com/About/Tiffany/clt.aspx

12. Young, Steve. (2002). *Great Failures of the Extremely Successful*. Los Angeles, CA: Tallfellow Press.

13. The Chronicle Of Coca-Cola. (2009). *Coca-Cola Company*. Retrieved from http://www.thecoca-colacompany.com/heritage/chronicle_birth_refreshing_idea.html

14. Sciaudone, C. (2004, May 21). This Test Taker Raised the Bar for Perseverance. *Los Angeles Times*. Retrieved from http://www.lawschool.com/48th.htm

15. Noah Webster, Writings and Biography. (2009). Retrieved from http://www.lexrex.com/bios/nwebster.htm

16. Durrett, M. (2009). The Life and Humor of Robin Williams. *About.com*. Retrieved from http://humor.about.com/od/comediansr/p/Robin_Williams. htm
17. Green, Joey. *Famous Failures*. (2007). Los Angeles, CA: Lunatic Press, p. 193.
18. Carleton, D. (2009, Dec 4). Cronkite's Texas: A Q&A with Walter Cronkite. *University of Texas at Austin - Know*. Retrieved from http://www.utexas.edu/know/2009/12/04/cronkites-texas-qa/
19. Van Ekeren, Glenn. (1994). *Speakers Sourcebook II*. Englewood Cliffs, NJ: Prentice Hall, p. 330.
20. Green, Joey. (2007). *Famous Failures*. Los Angeles, CA: Lunatic Press, p. 260.
21. Sandra Day O'Connor Gives Third Annual William French Smith Memorial Lecture. (2009, March 27). Pepperdine University School of Law. Retrieved from http://law.pepperdine.edu/news-events/news/2009/03/oconnor.htm
22. Green, Joey. (2007). *Famous Failures*. Los Angeles, CA: Lunatic Press, p. 280.

Chapter 10:   Feels Like You're Getting Nowhere

Chapter 11:   A Whole Mess 'O Stress

1. Gillanders, Ann. (1995). *Joy of Reflexology*. London: Gaia Books Limited.
2. Khurana, S. (2010). Positive Quotes. *About.com*. Retrieved from http://quotations.about.com/cs/inspirationquotes/a/Optimism8.htm
3. Hillukka, T. (2010, Jan 23). The Psychology of Color: Calming Colors that Will Soothe Your Senses. *Associated Content*. Retrieved from http://www.associatedcontent.com/article/2624235/the_psychology_of_color_calming_colors_pg2.html?cat=30
4. Lawson, Willow. (2003, Feb 4). Eat Right To Fight Stress. *Psychology Today Magazine*. Retrieved from http://psychologytoday.com/articles/pto-20030204-000003.html
5. Clark, Ron J. *Personal Fitness Trainer Study and Reference Manual*. Lafayette, IN: National Federation of Professional Trainers. 2002.
6. Healthy Sleep Tips. (2007). *National Sleep Foundation*. Retrieved from http://www.sleepfoundation.org/site/c.huIXKjM0IxF/b.2419247/k.BCB0/Healthy_Sleep_Tips.htm
7. Paul MacCready. (2010). *Academy of Achievement*. Retrieved from Retrieved from http://www.achievement.org/autodoc/page/mac0int-1
8. Editors of Publications International. (2010, Aug 17). 14 Best-Selling Books Repeatedly Rejected by Publishers. *In How Stuff Works*. Retrieved from http://entertainment.howstuffworks.com/arts/literature/14-best-selling-books-repeatedly-rejected-by-publishers.htm

Chapter 12:   A Healthy Balance

1. Hardly Famous - What they did before they were famous. (2010). Retrieved from http://www.hardlyfamous.com/

Chapter 13:   Walk With Determination

1. Edutopia: What Works in Public Education. (2008, Mar 3). Charles Best: Connecting Dollars to Classrooms. *The George Lucas Educational Foundation.* Retrieved from http://www.edutopia.org/charles-best#
2. Armless Teen Drummer A Drumming Competition Finalist. (2007, Feb 5). *Impact Lab.* Retrieved from http://www.impactlab.com/2007/02/05/armless-teen-drummer-a-drumming-competition-finalist/
3. Bryant, Gay (Ed.). (2006, Summer). Survey: Most Important Element for Success. Success Magazine, 49, 88.
4. Susan Butcher. (2010). *Academy of Achievement.* Retrieved from http://www.achievement.org/autodoc/steps/per?index=17
5. Jonas Salk. (2010). *Academy of Achievement.* Retrieved from http://www.achievement.org/autodoc/page/sal0int-2
6. Kersey, Cynthia. (2005). *Unstoppable.* Naperville, IL: Sourcebooks, p. 119.